Girl's Drawing

사부작 사부작 소녀의 드로잉

Coloring Book

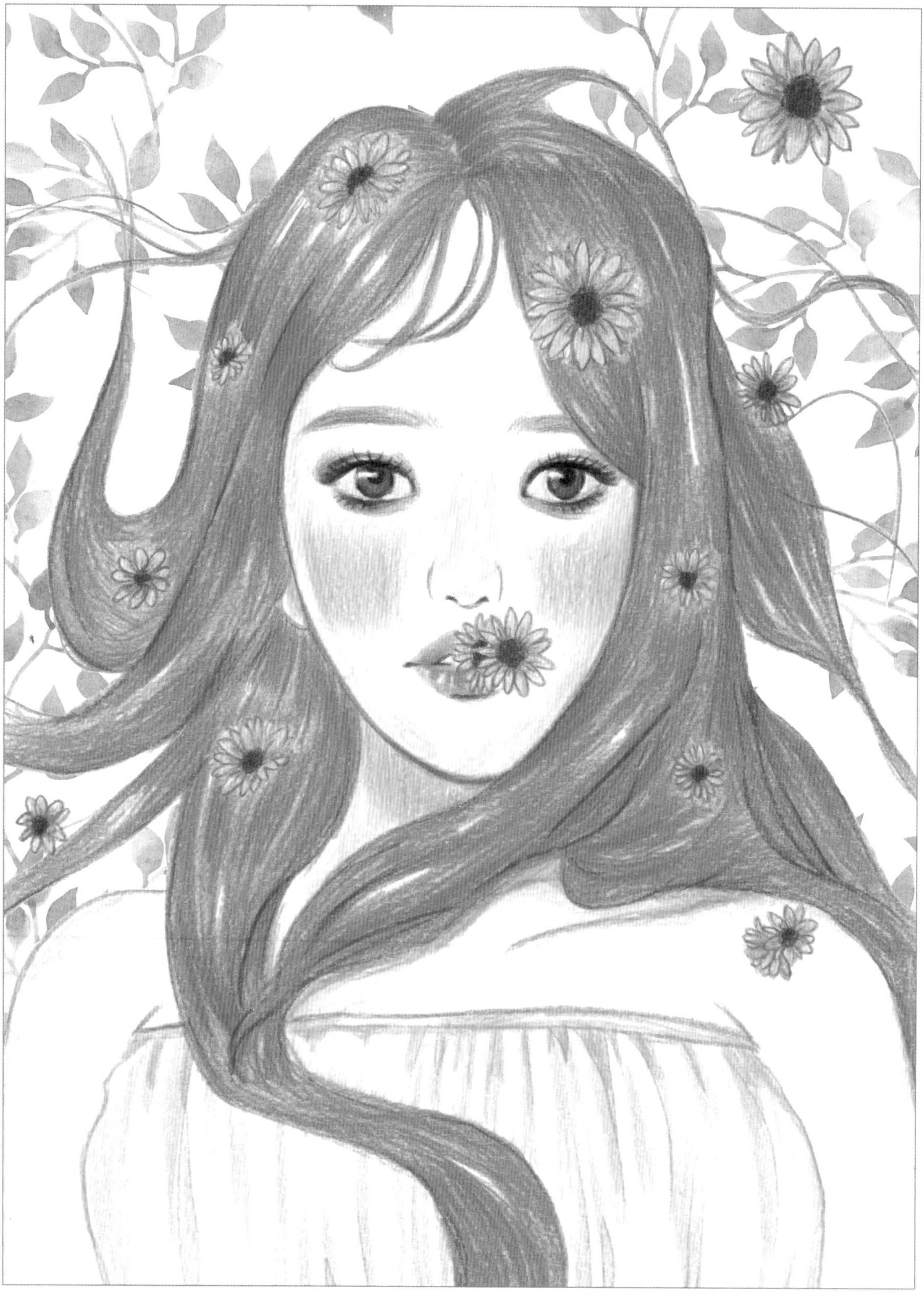

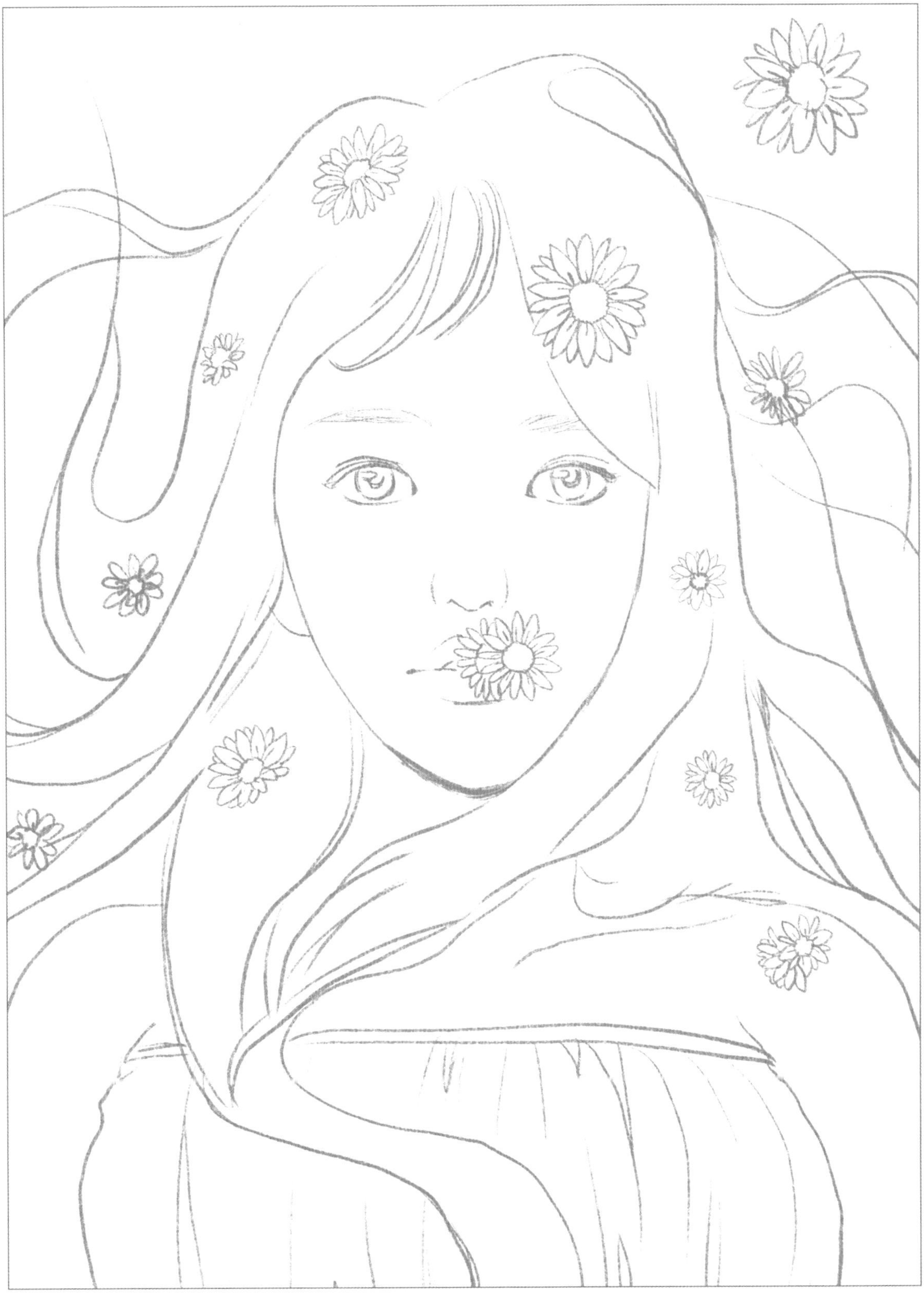

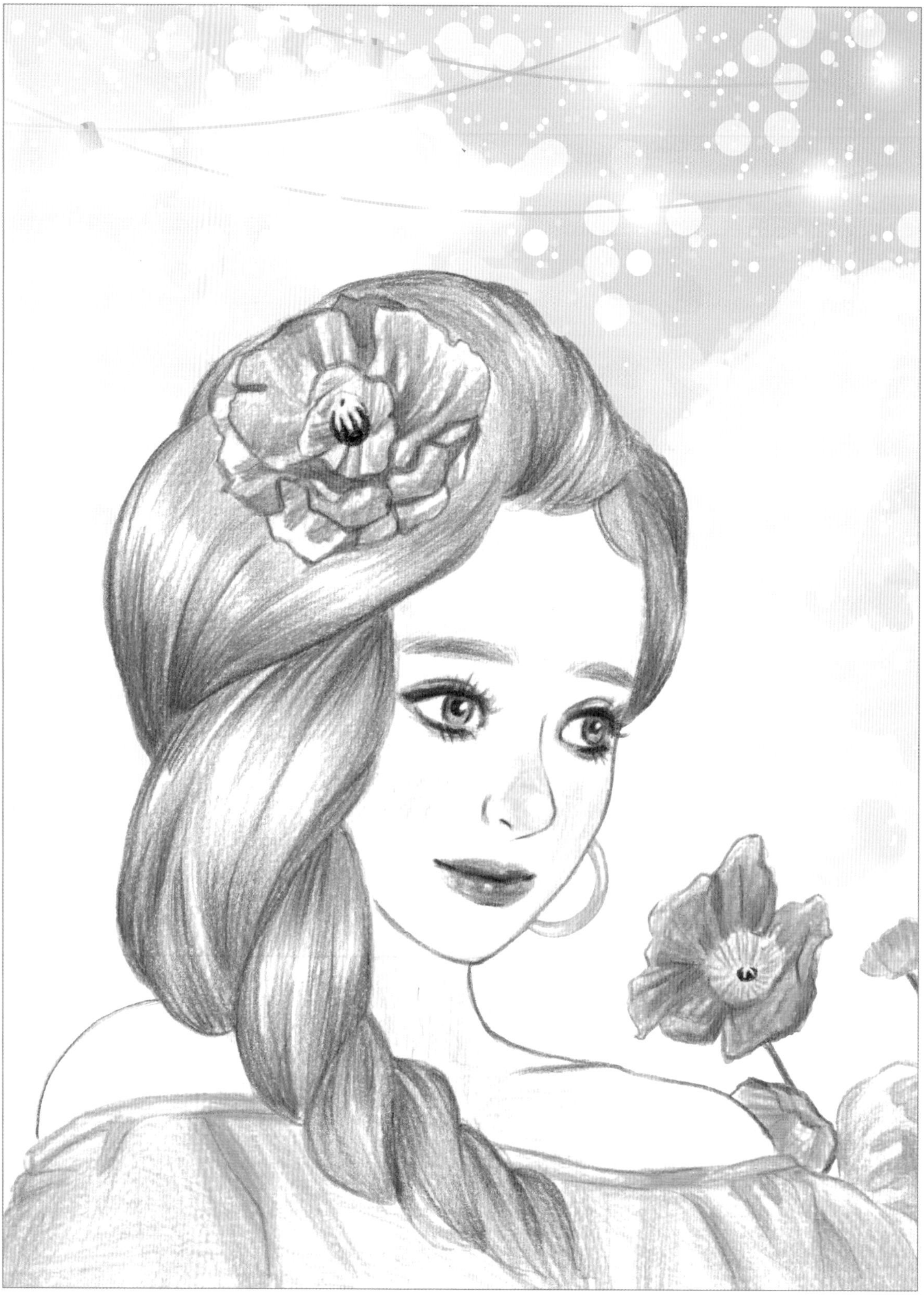

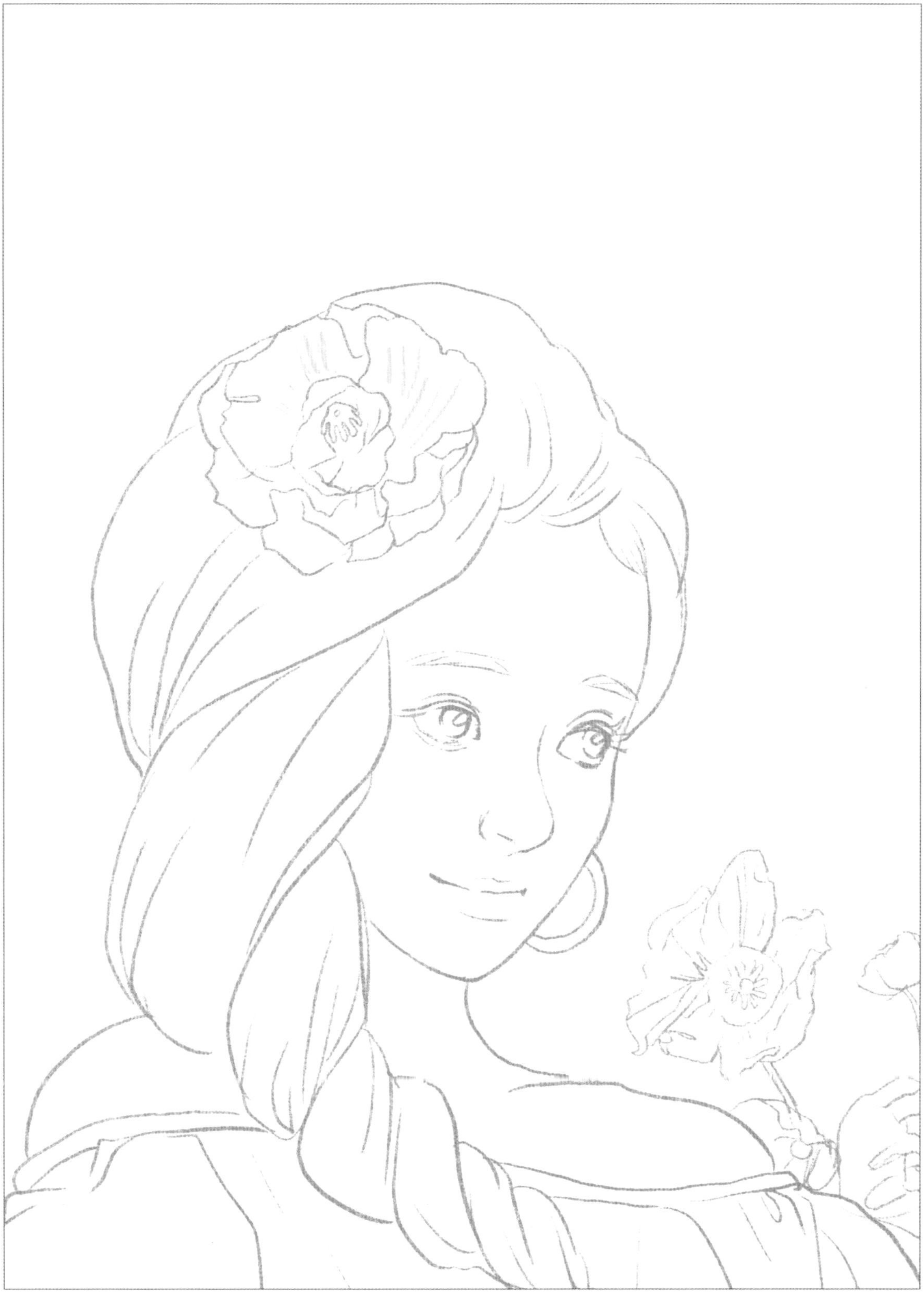

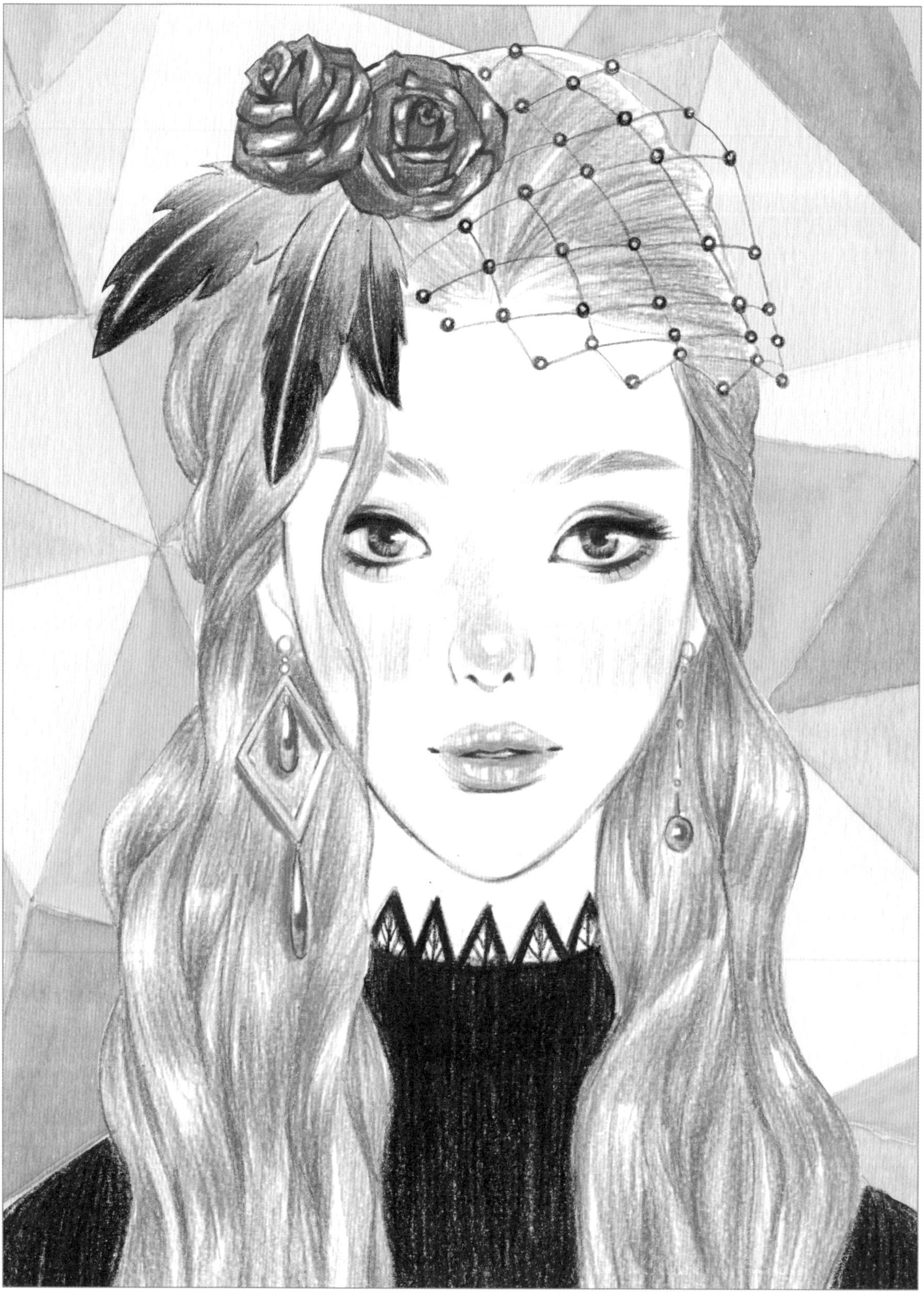

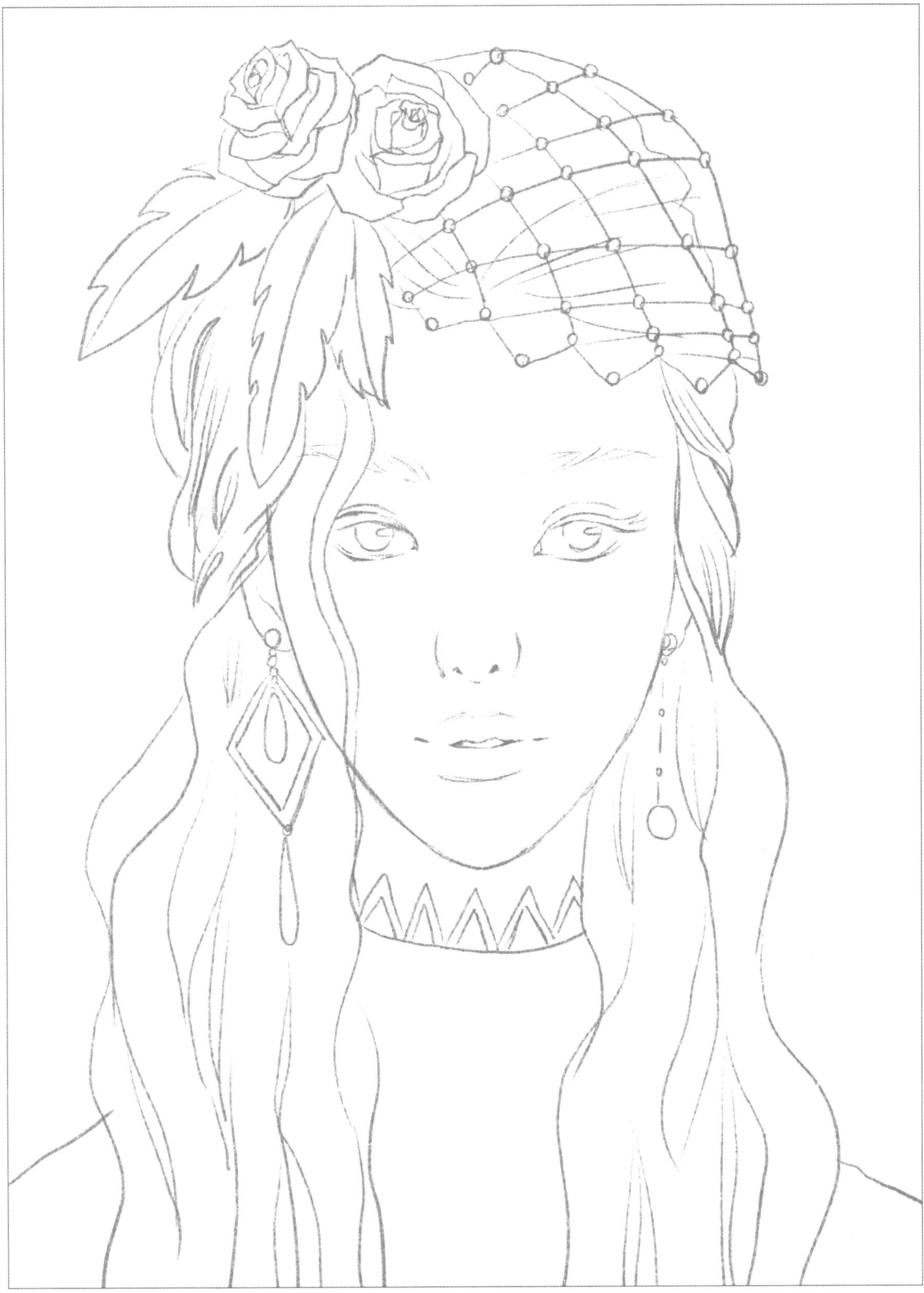

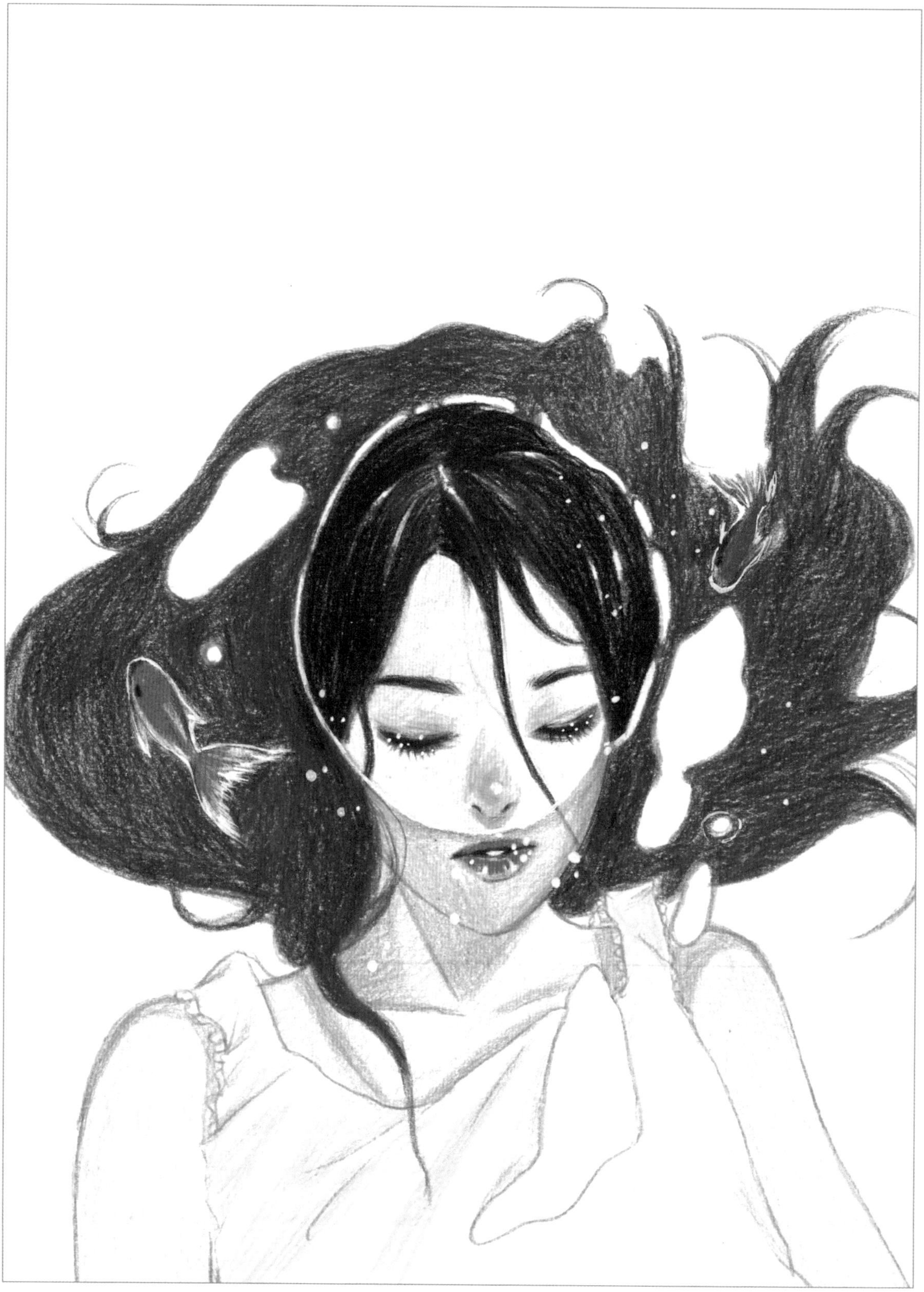

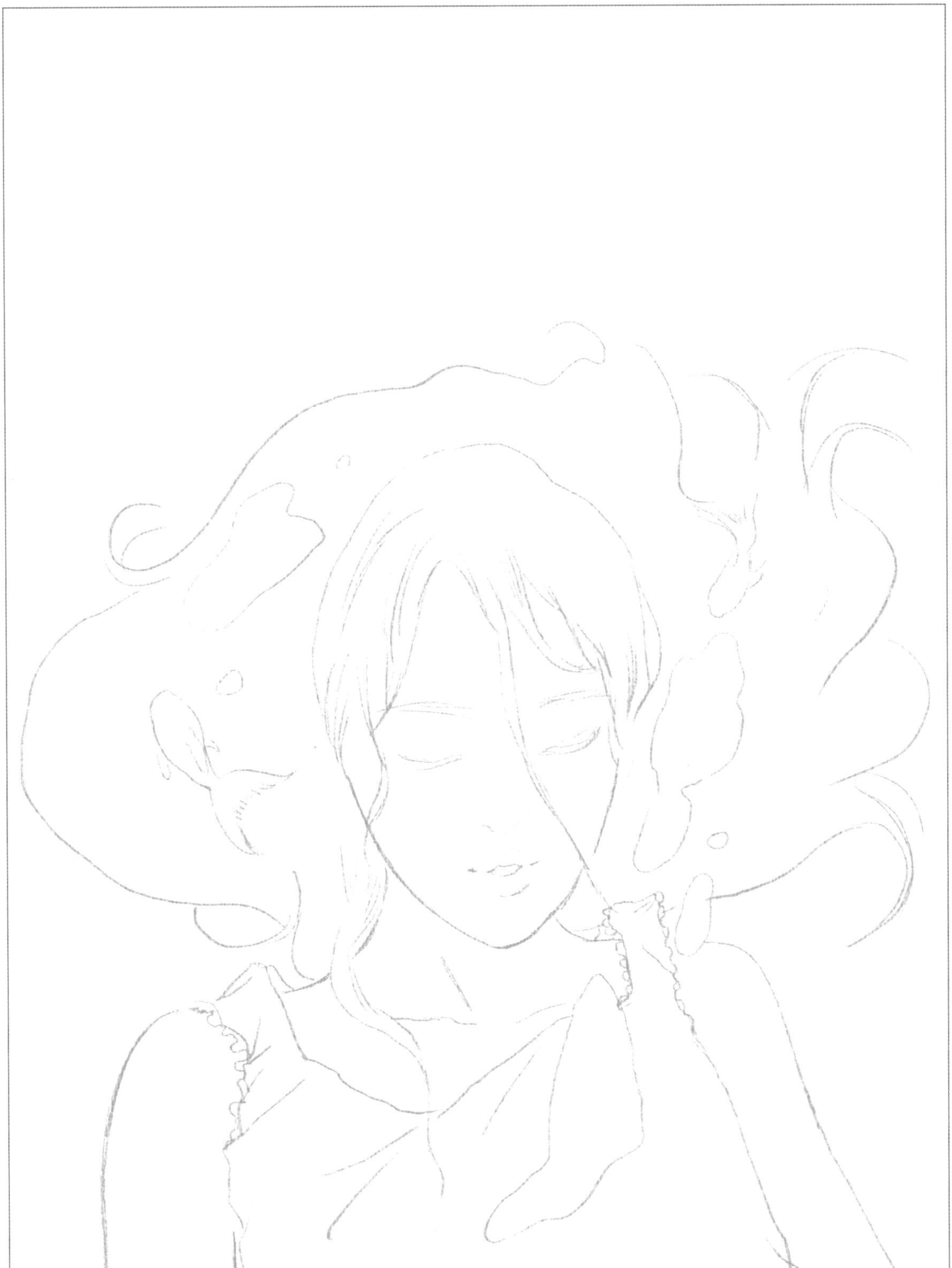

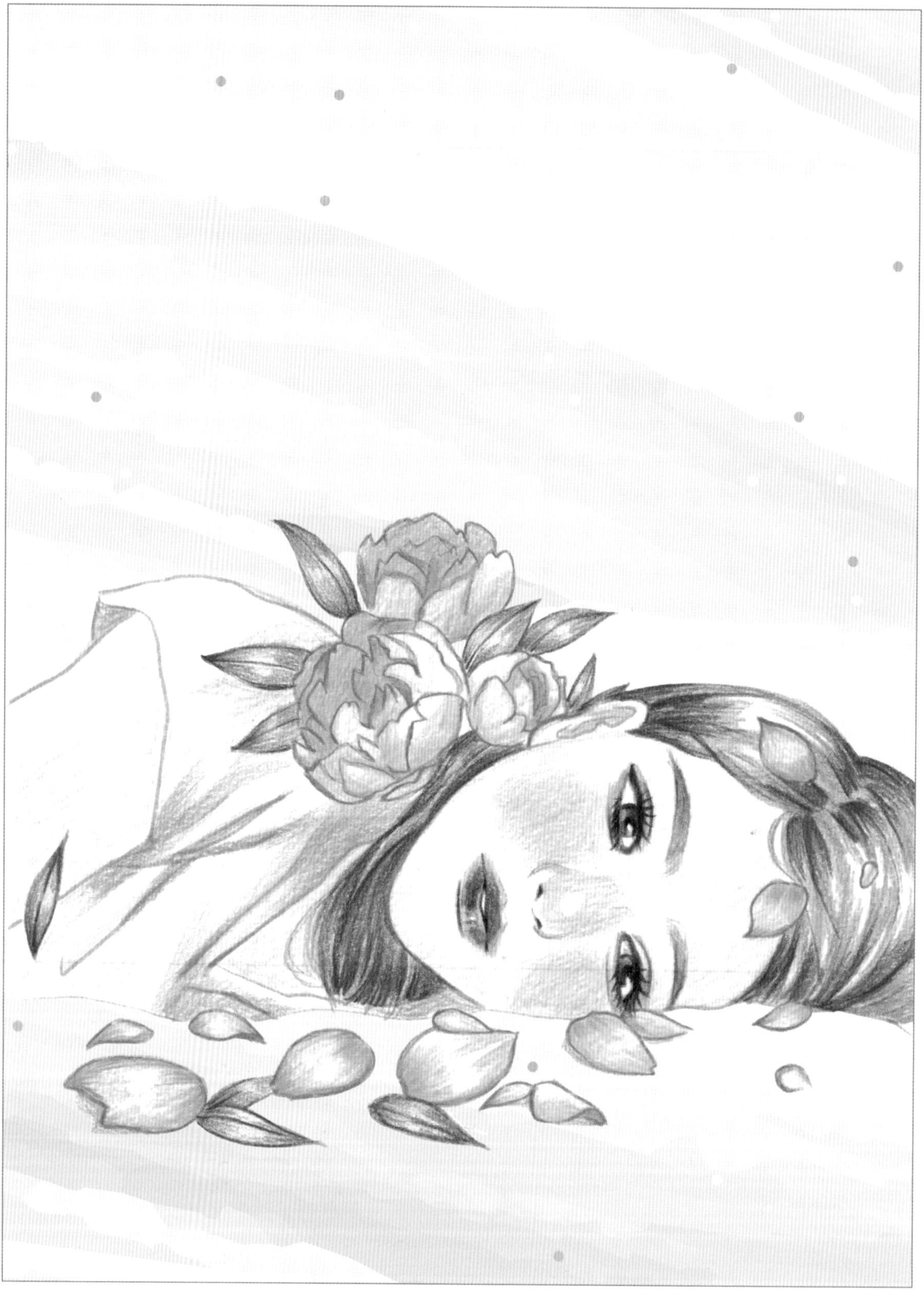

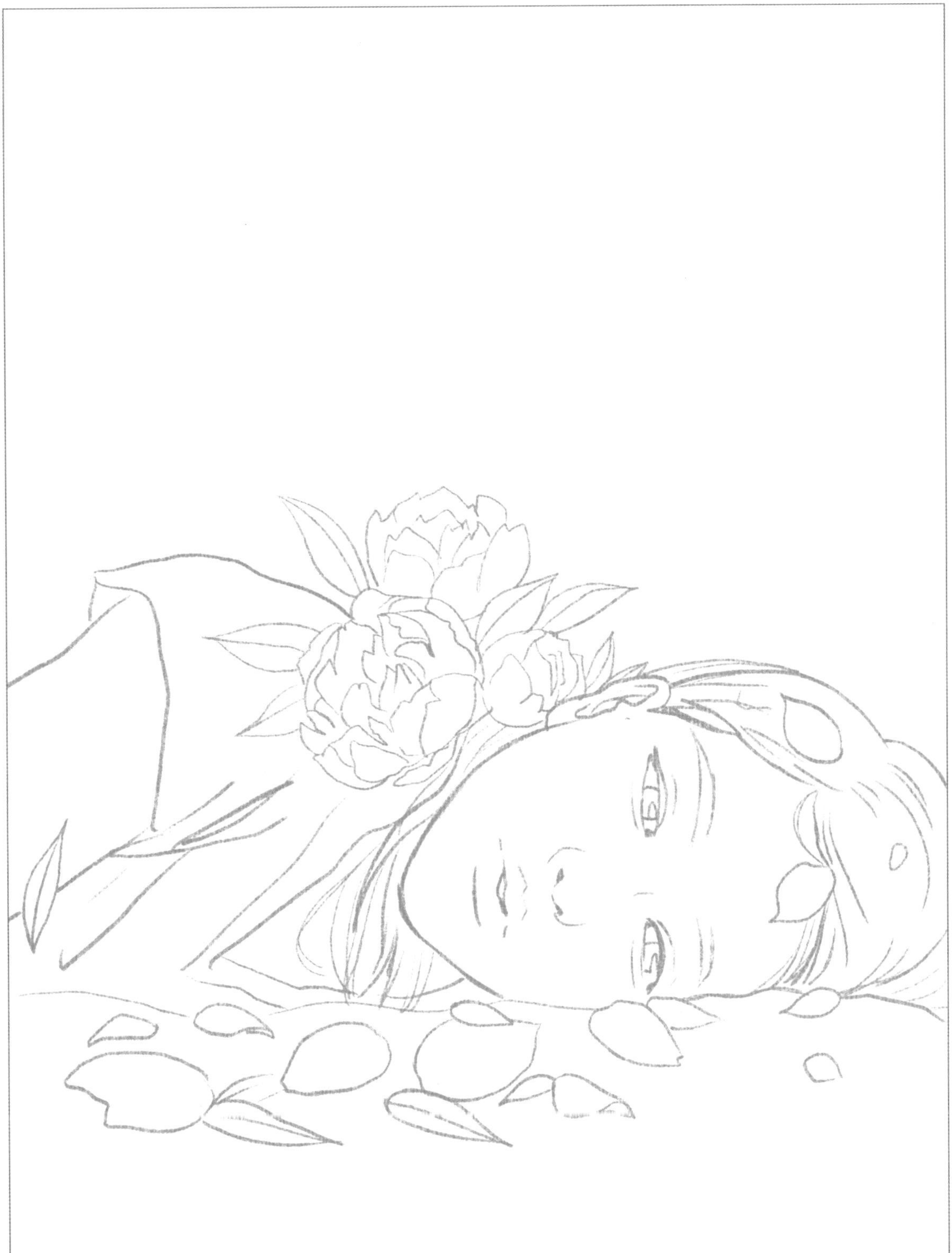

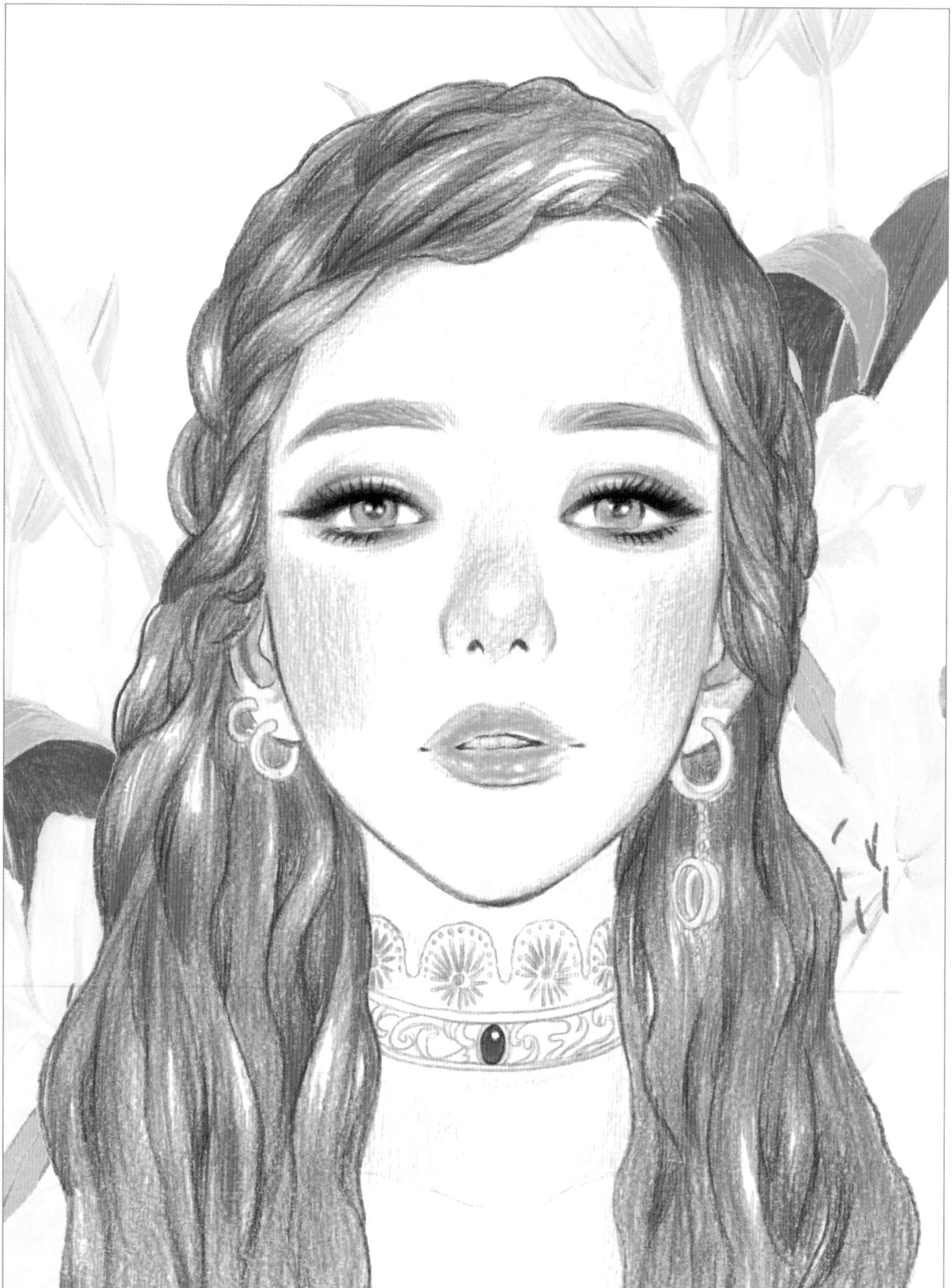

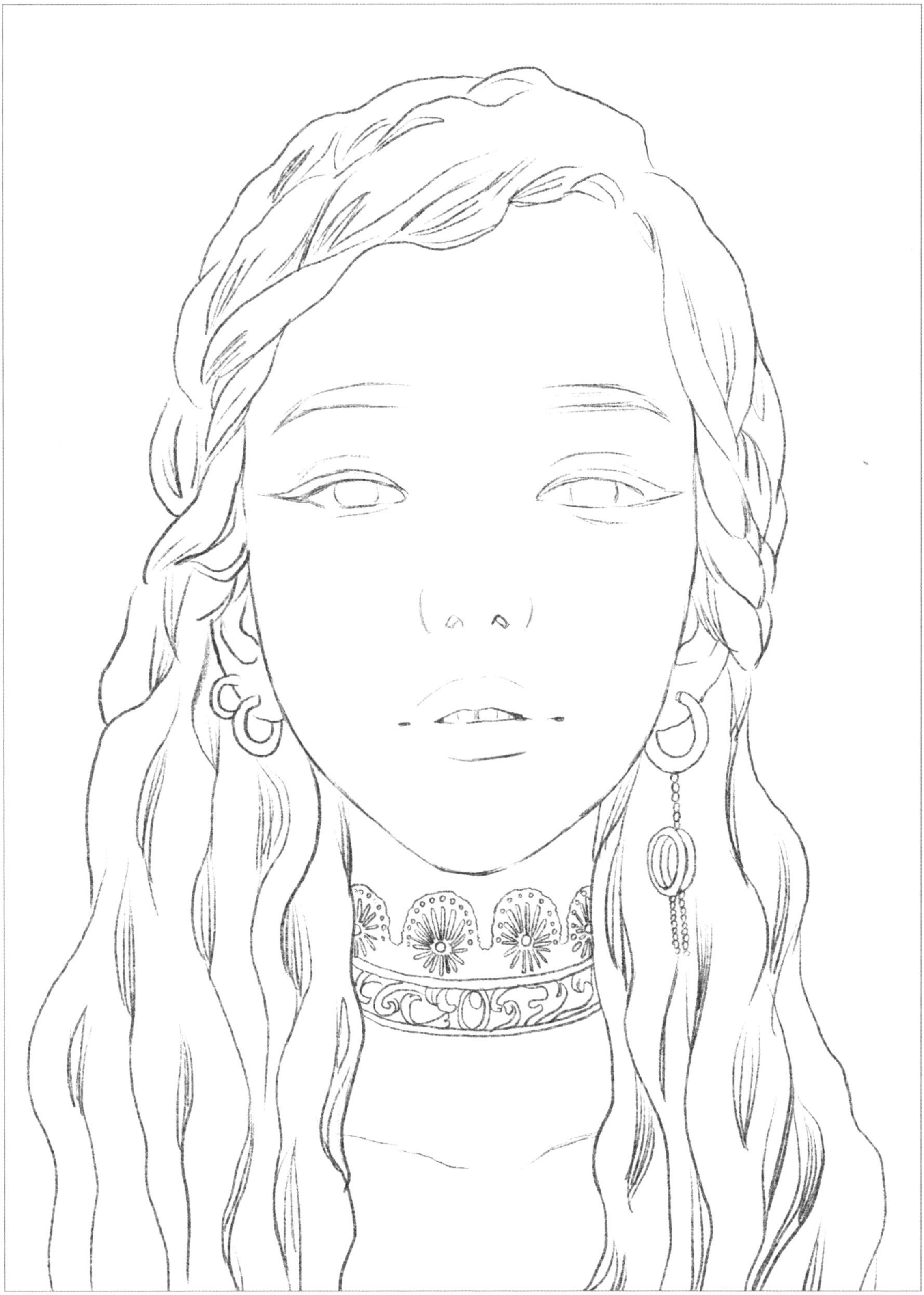

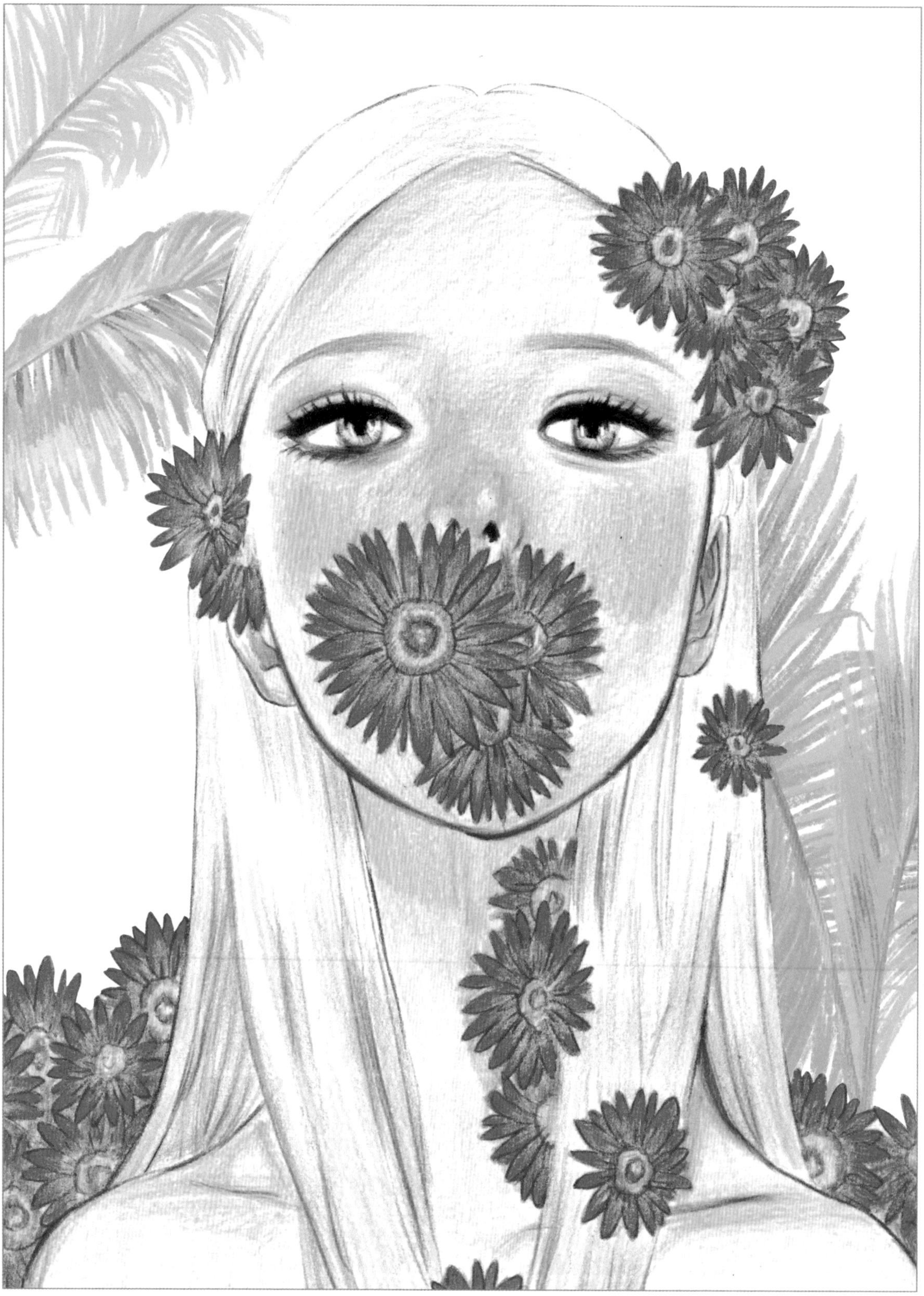

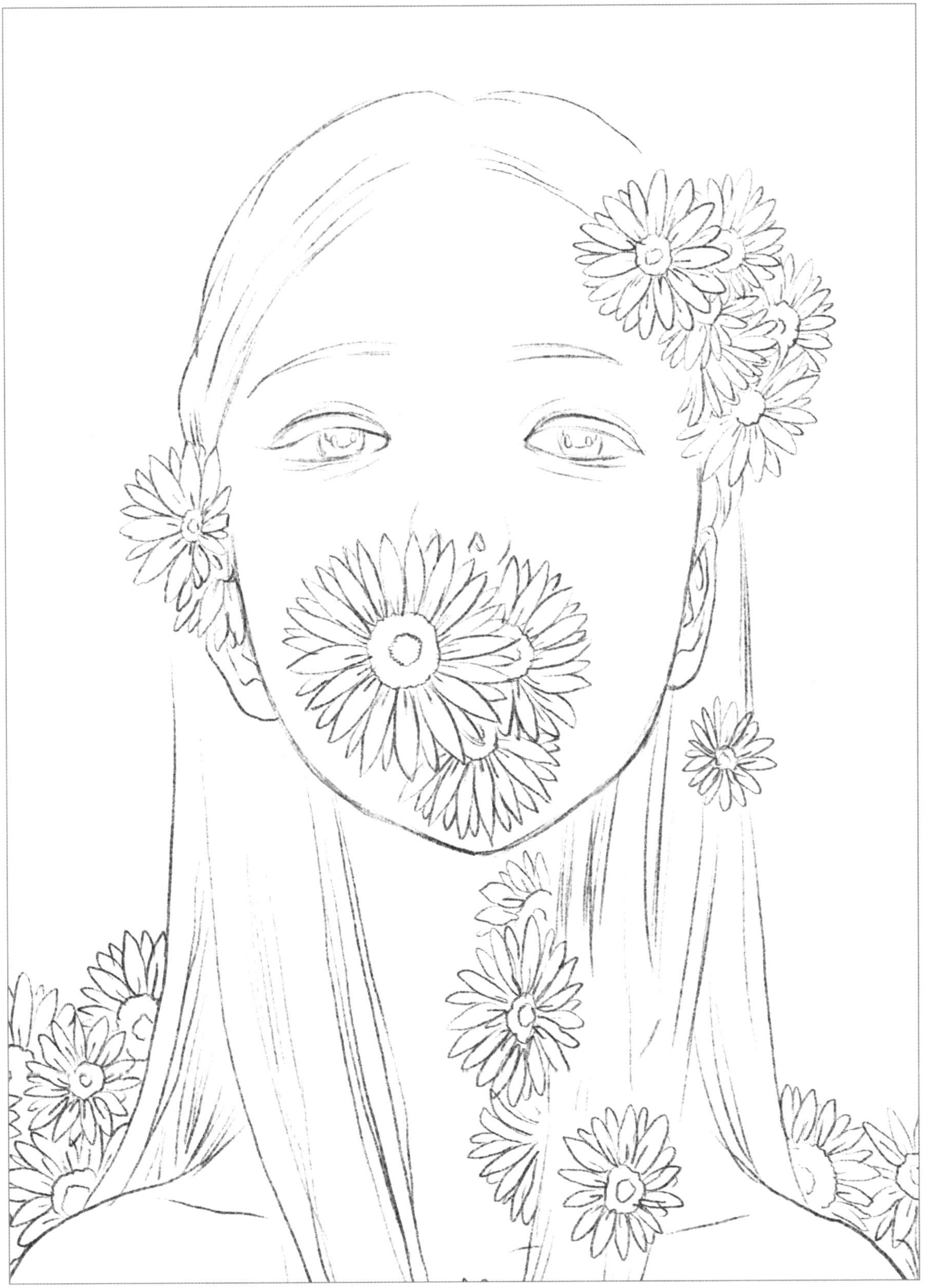

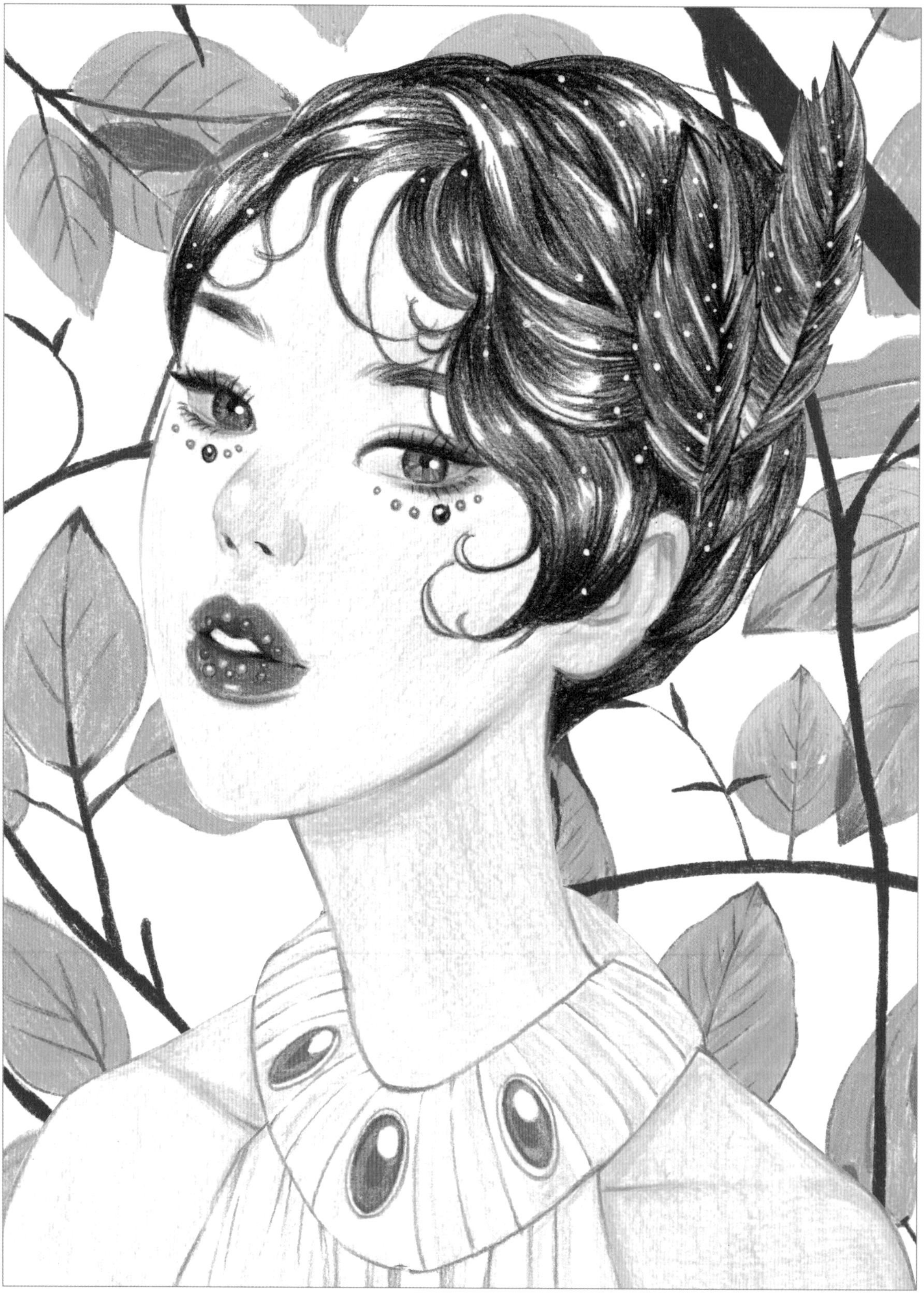

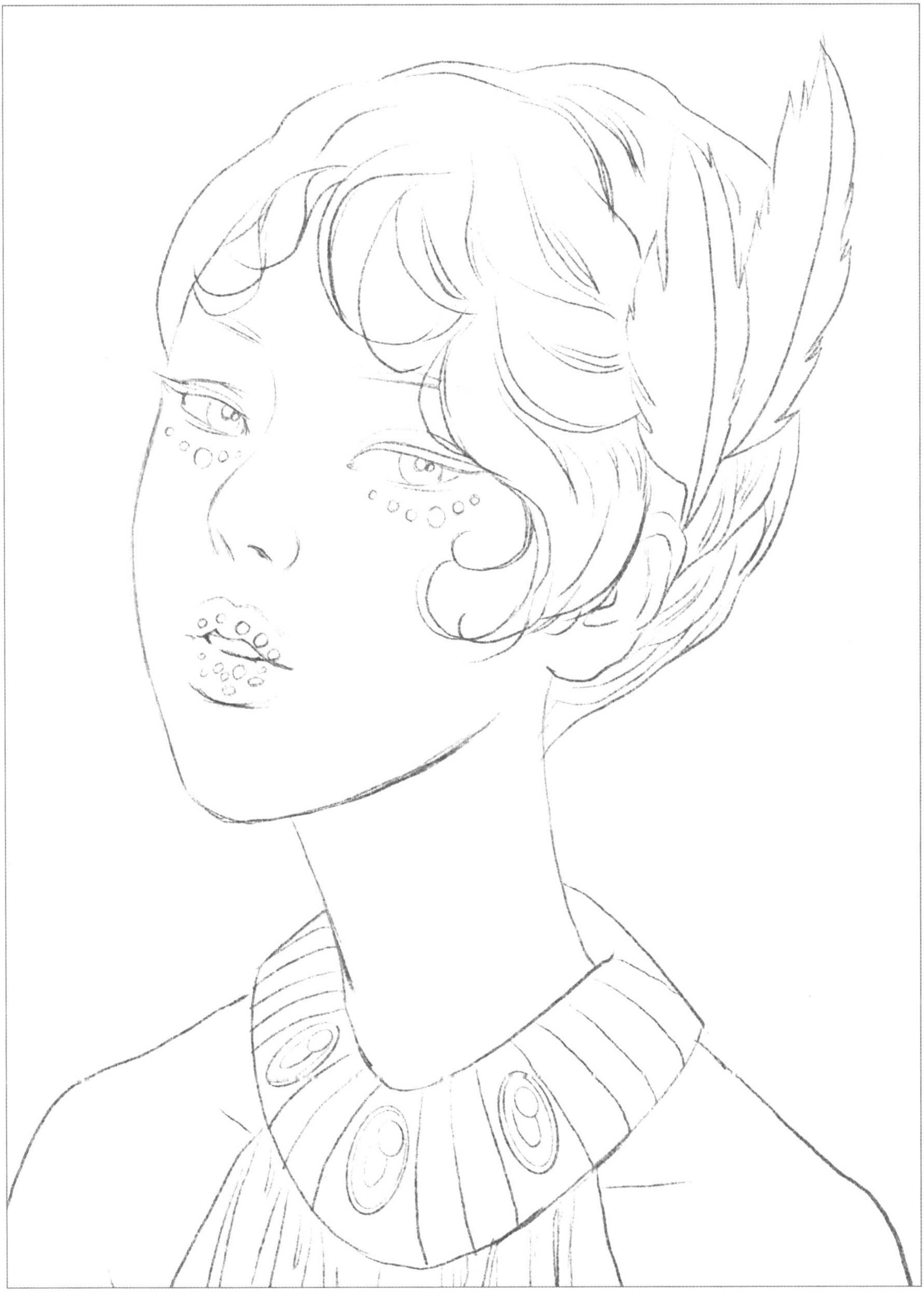

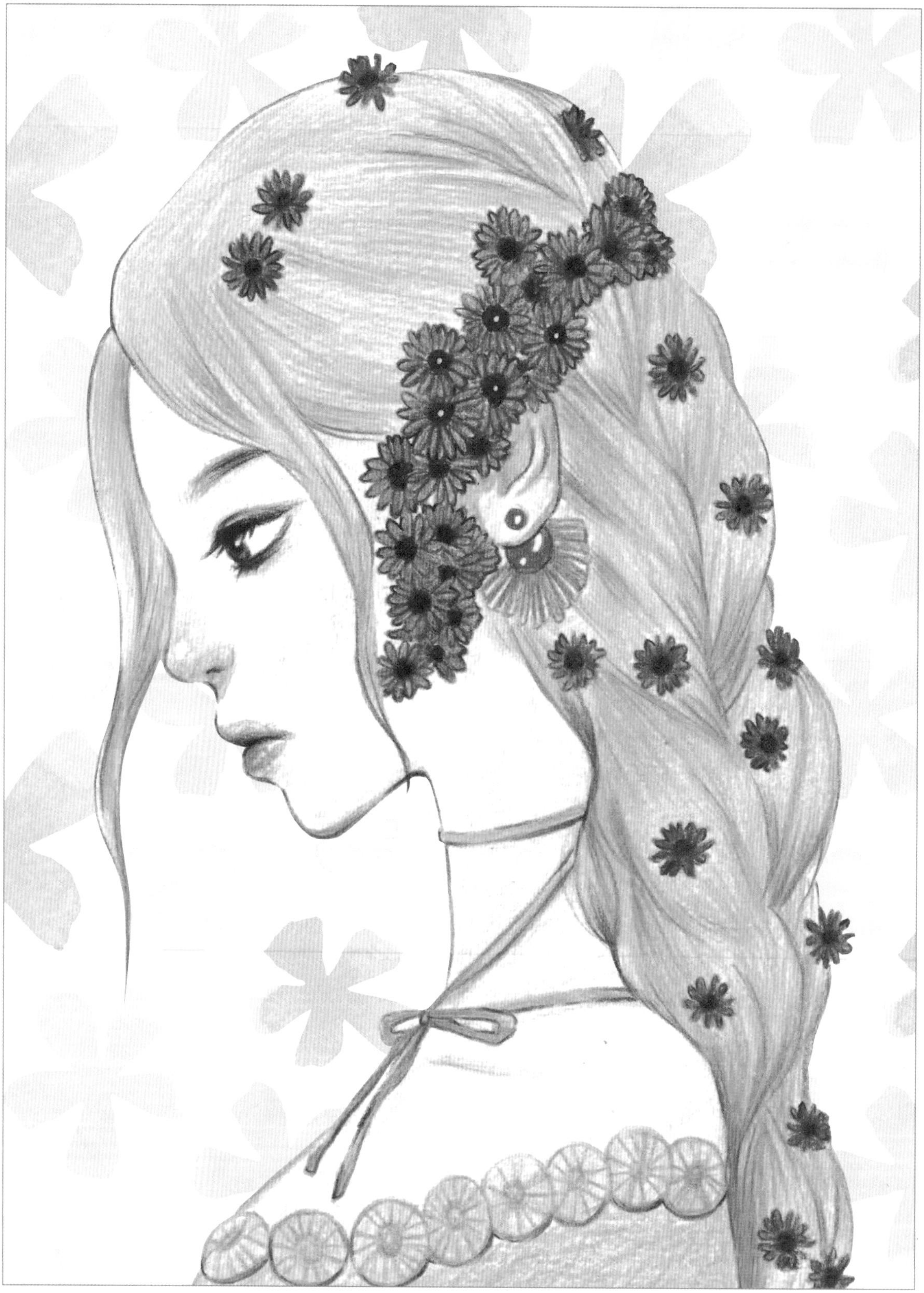

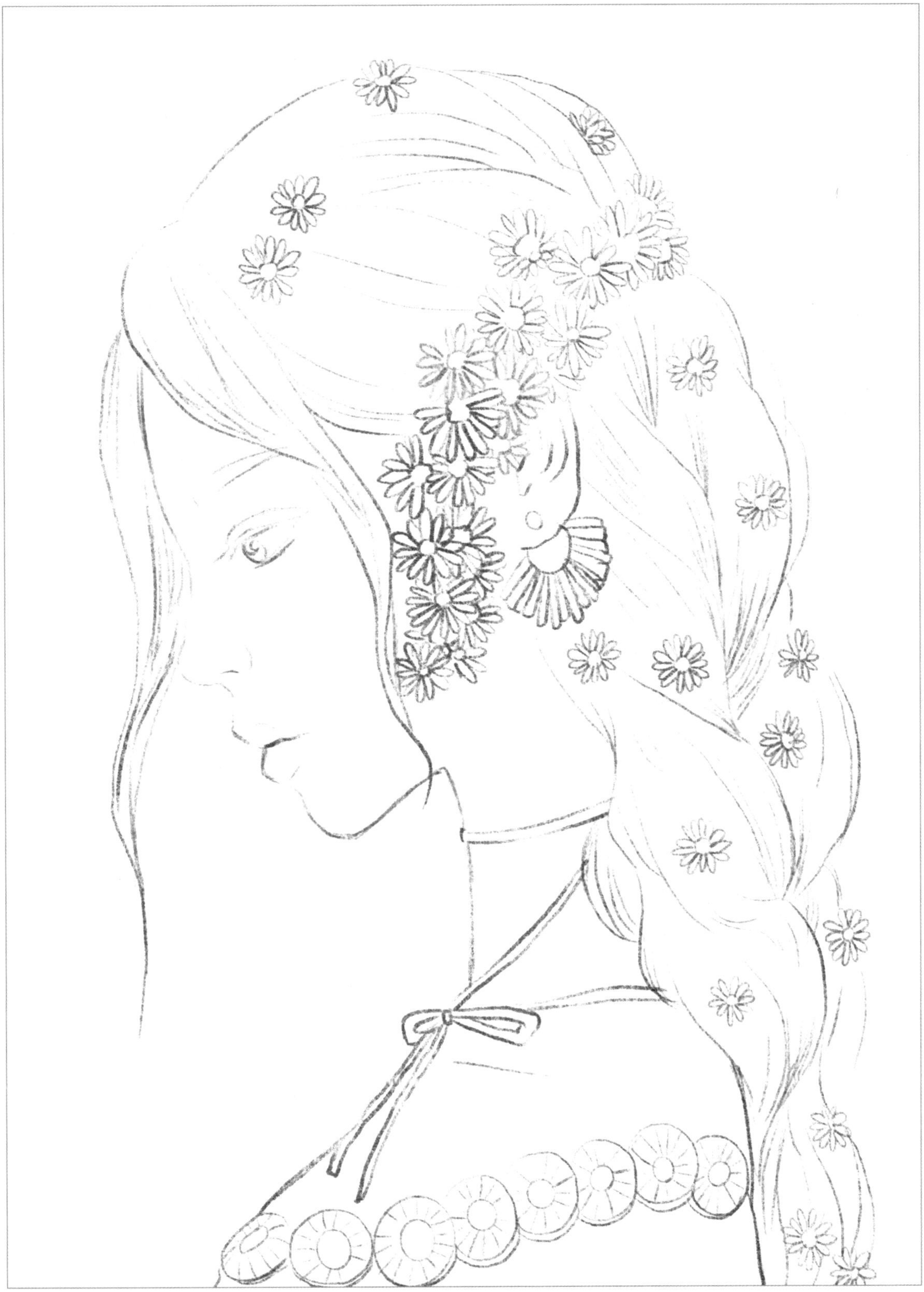

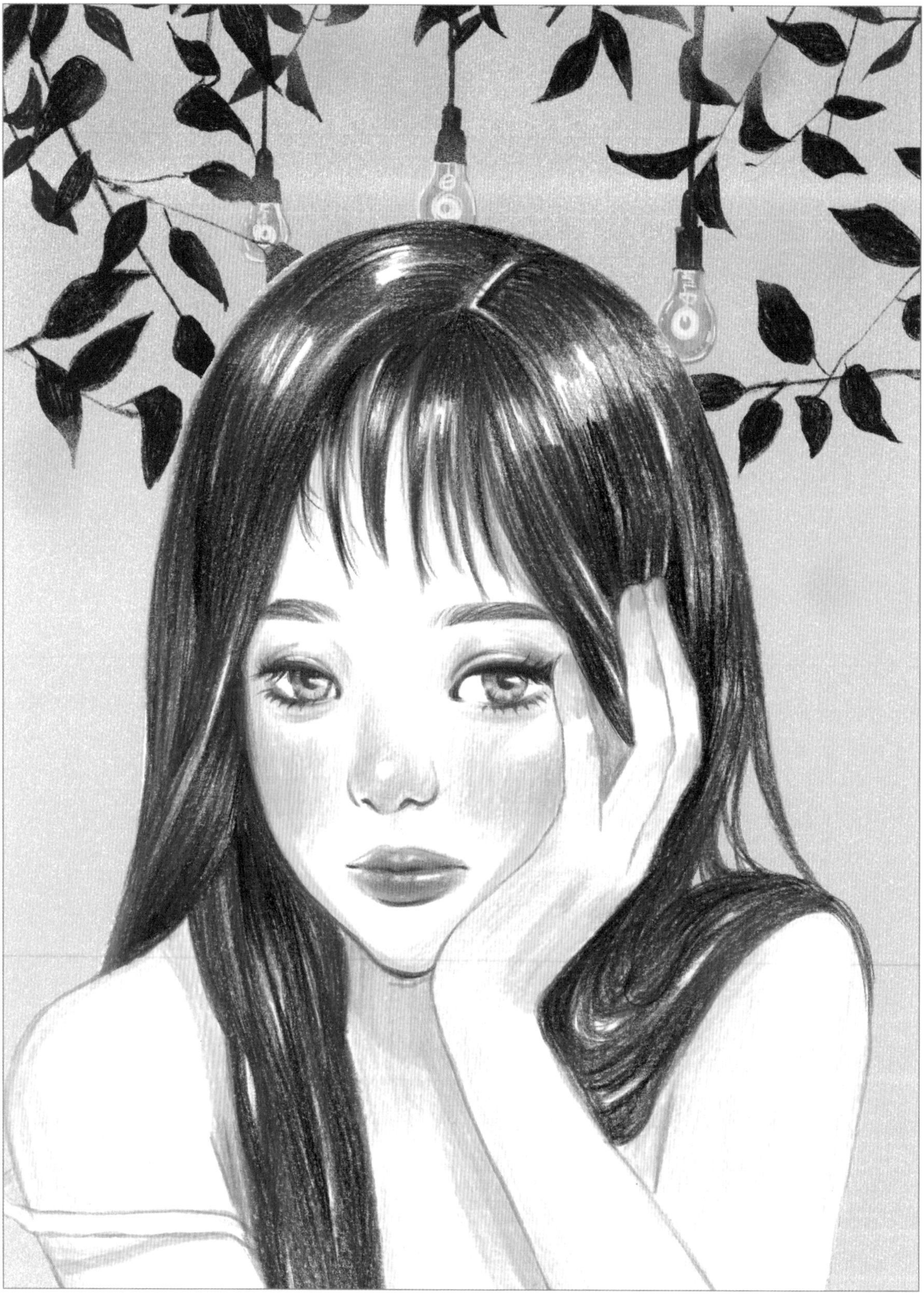

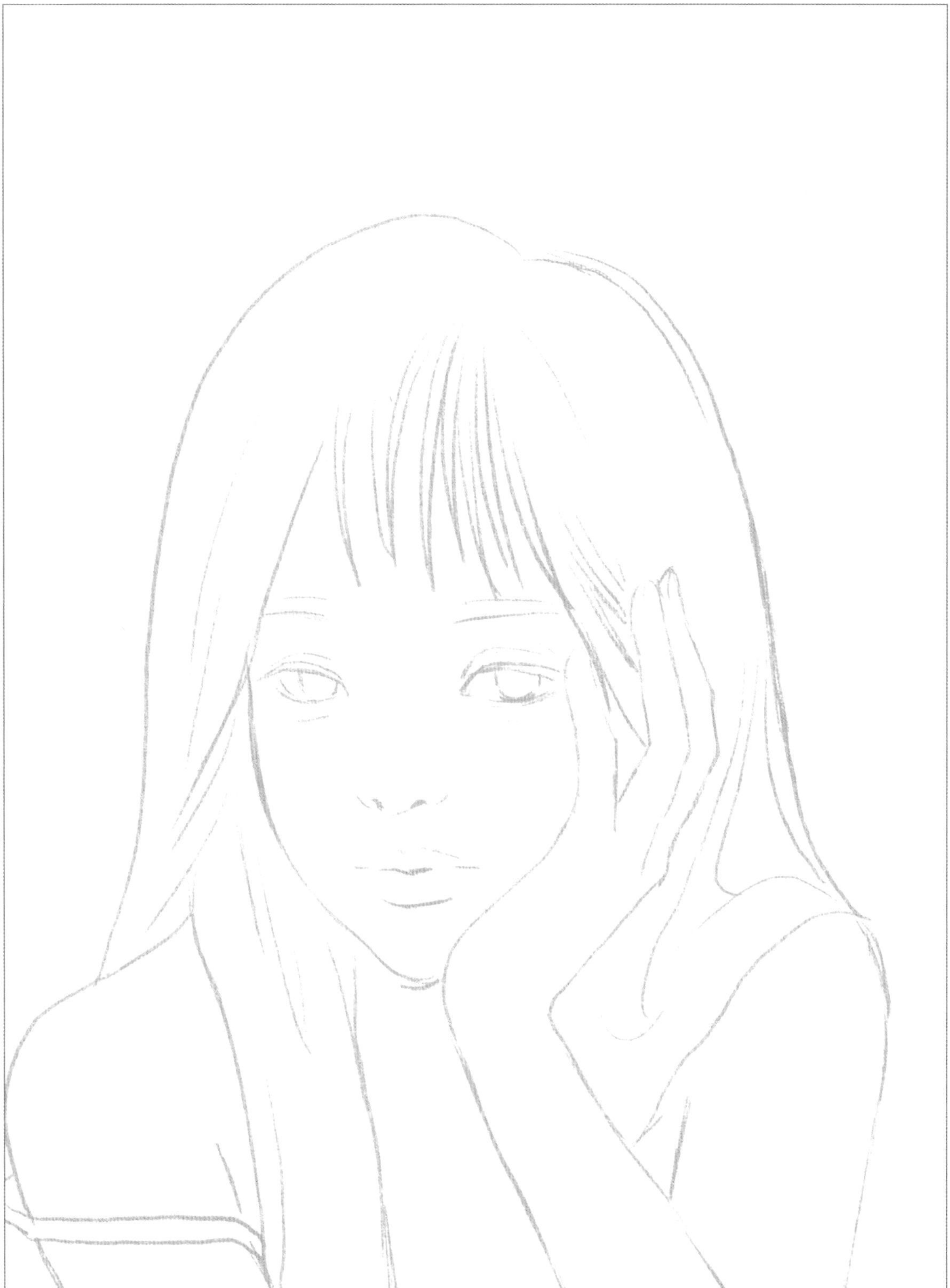

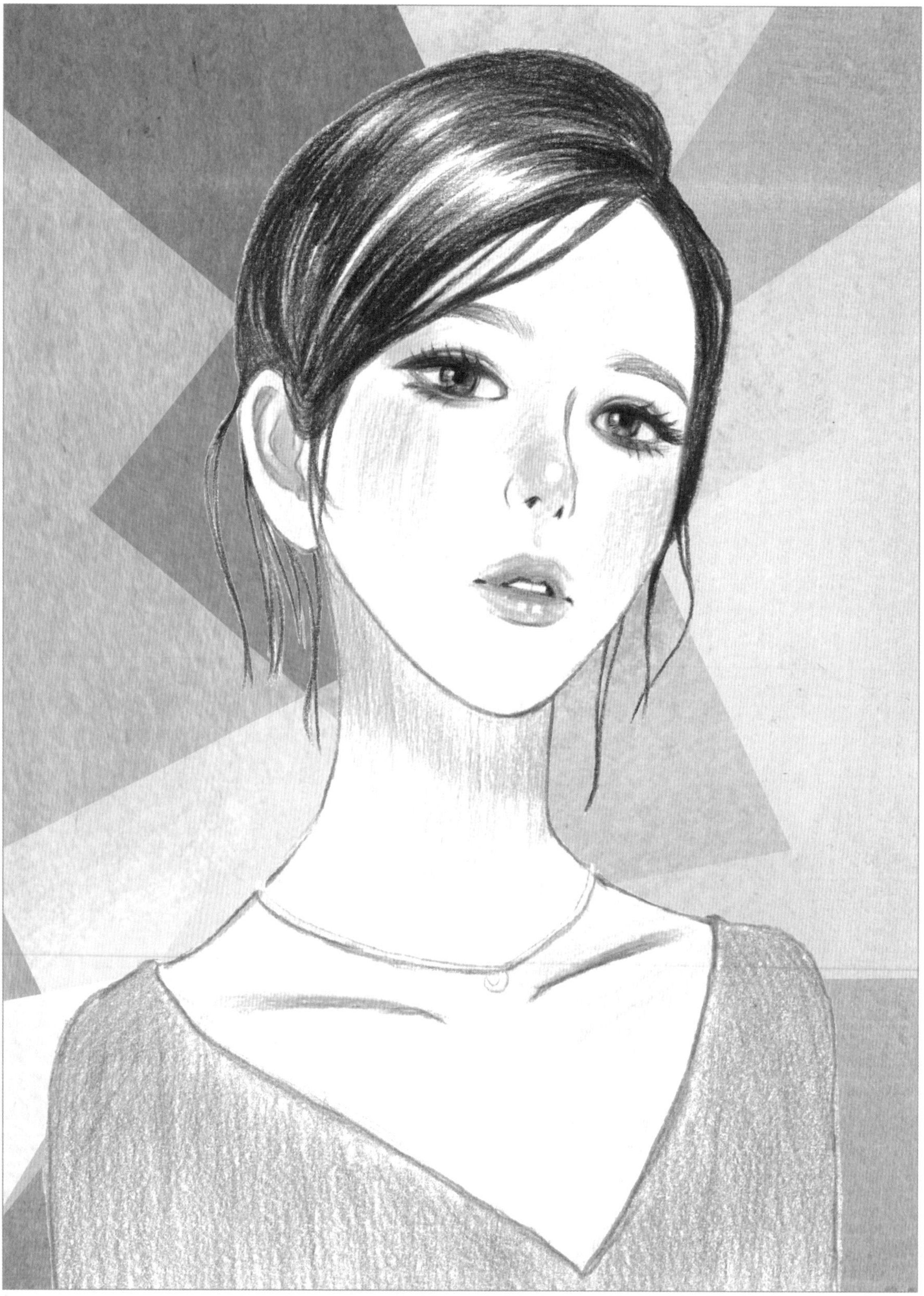

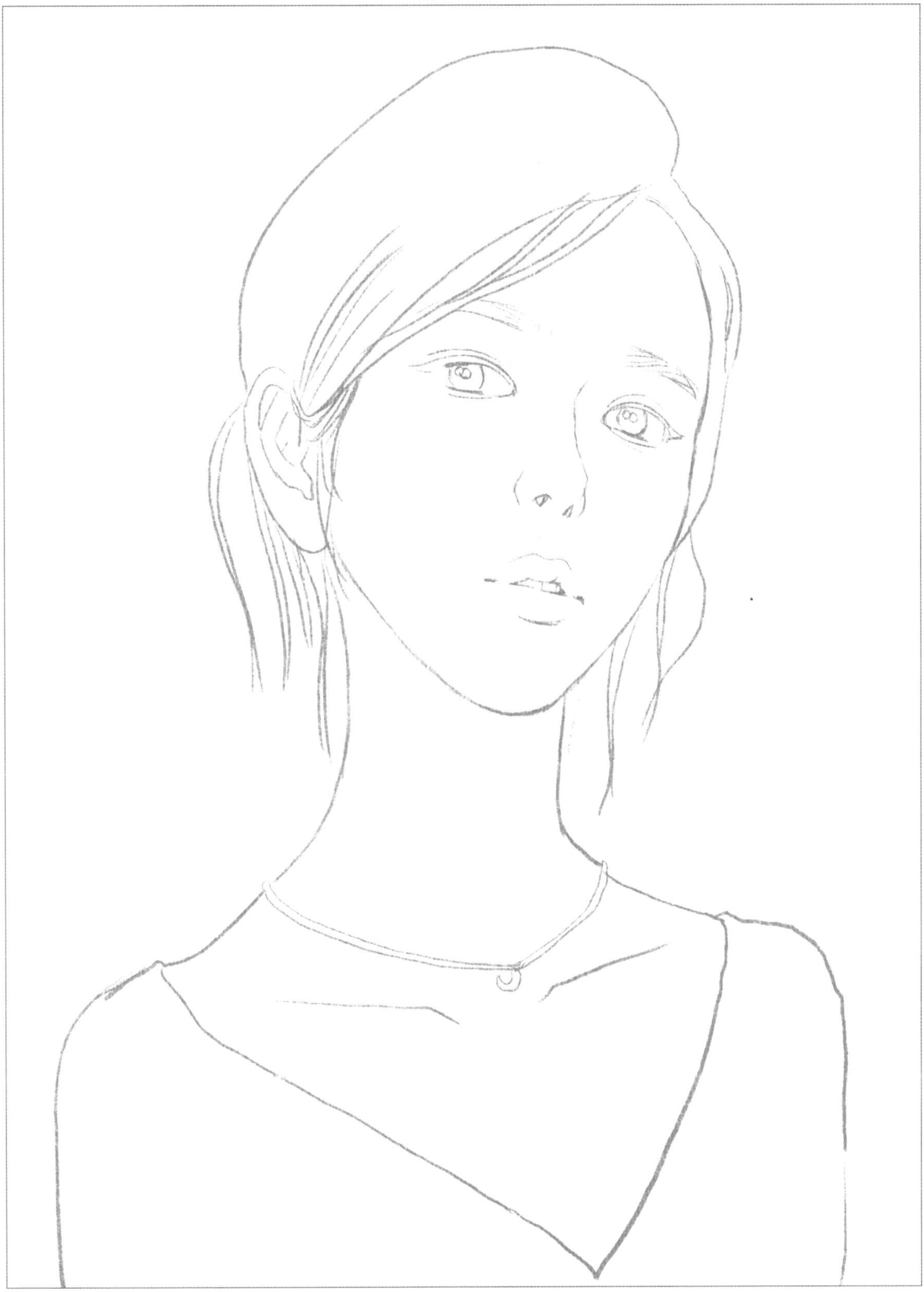

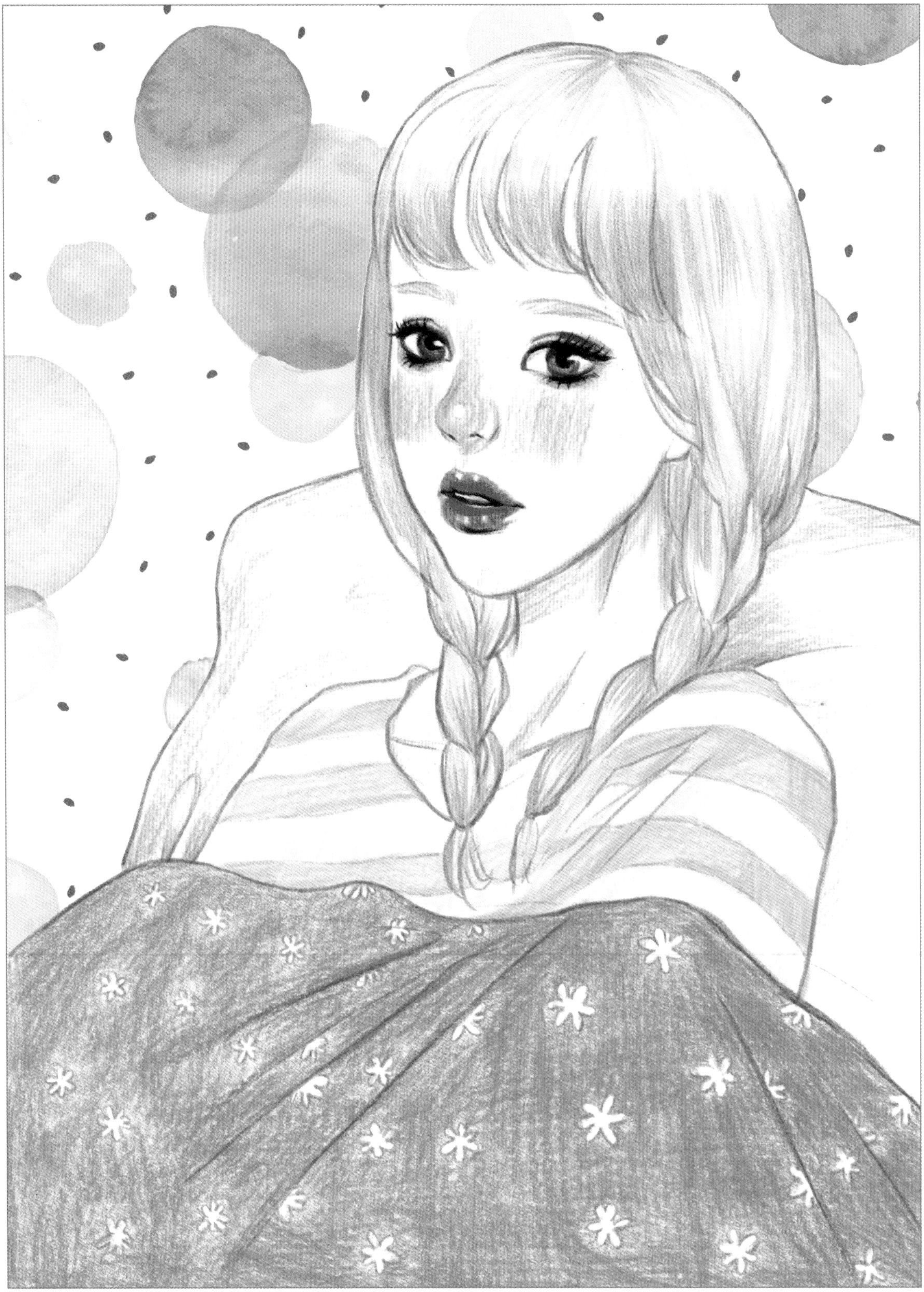

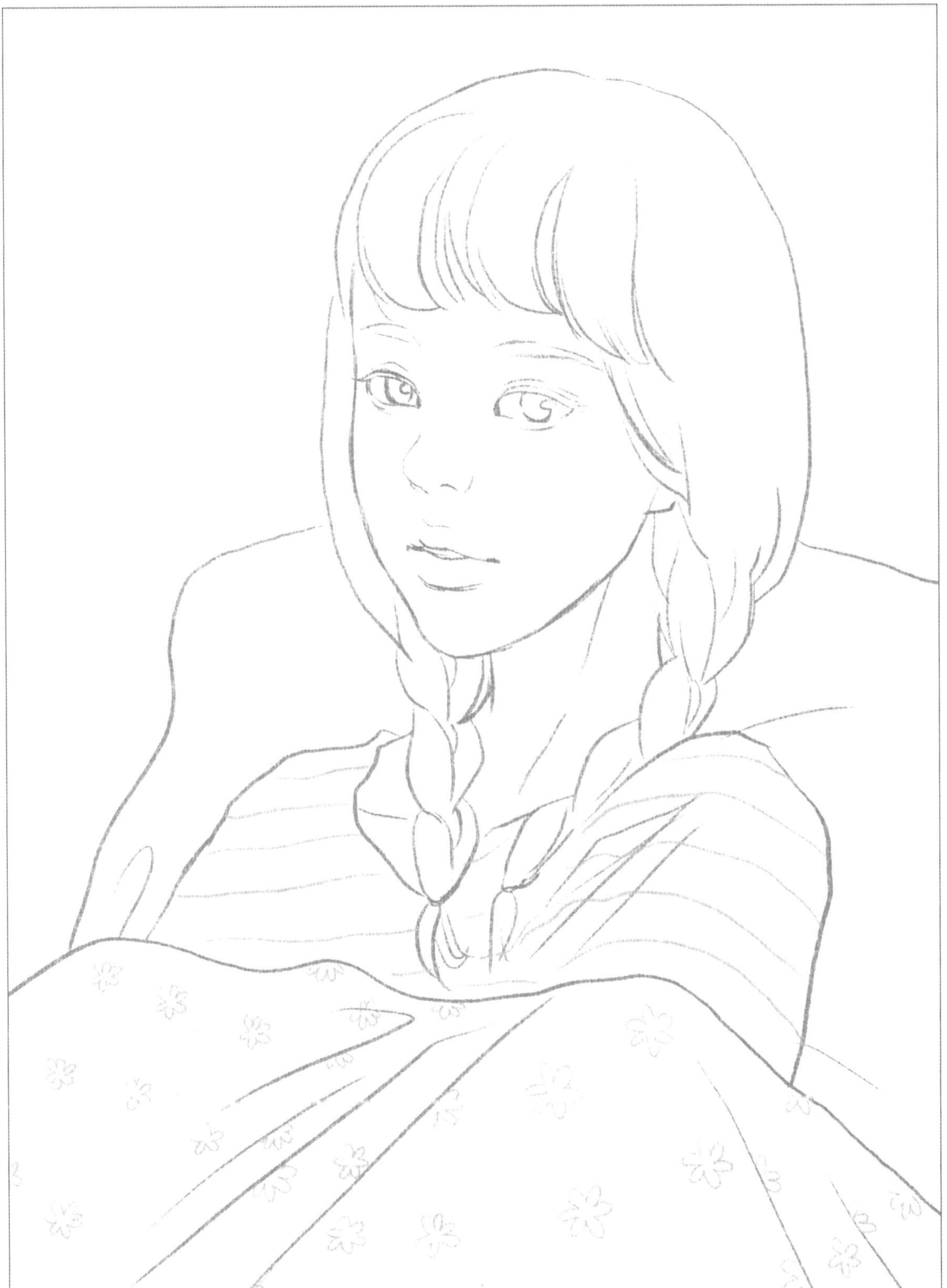

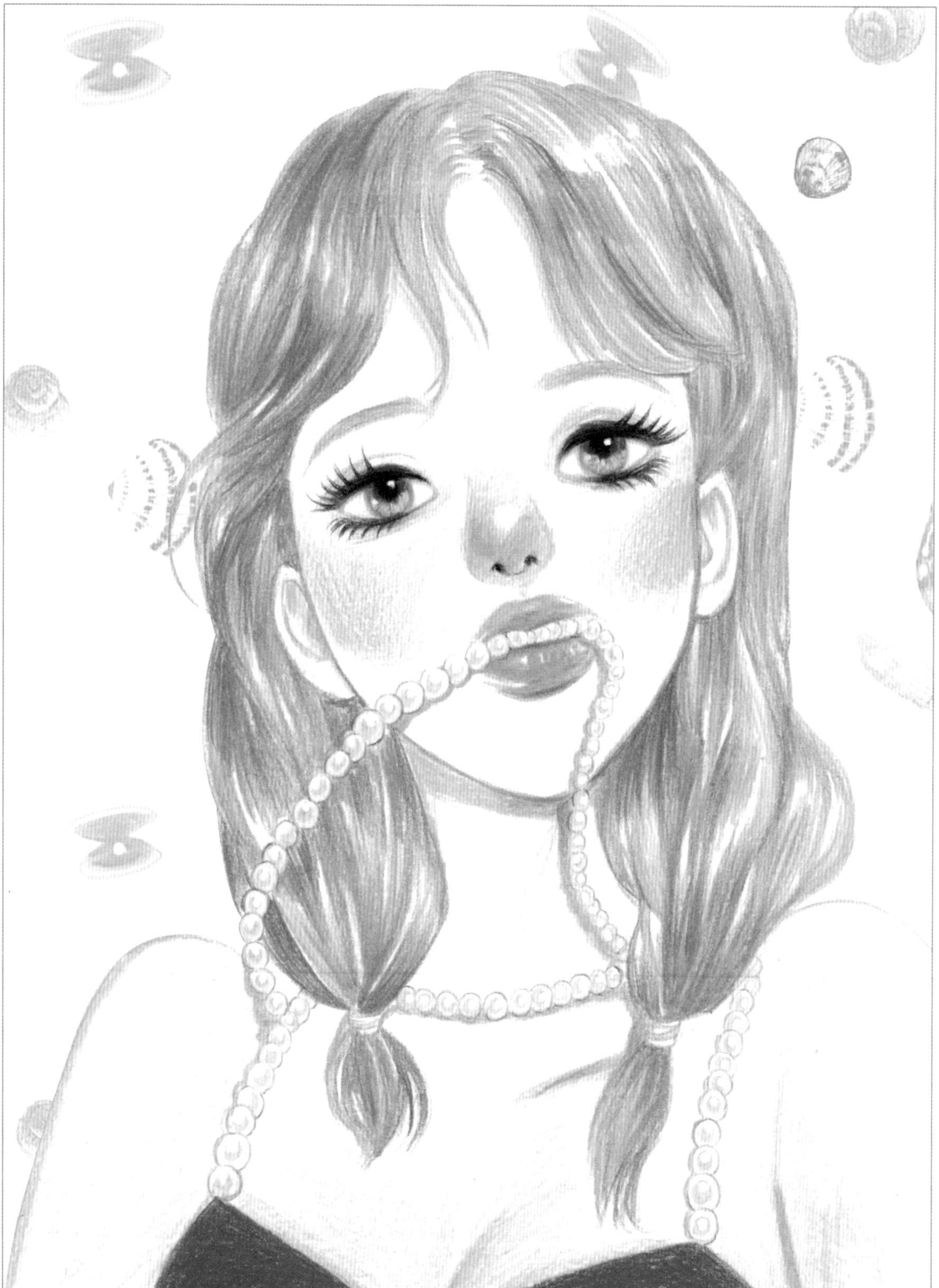

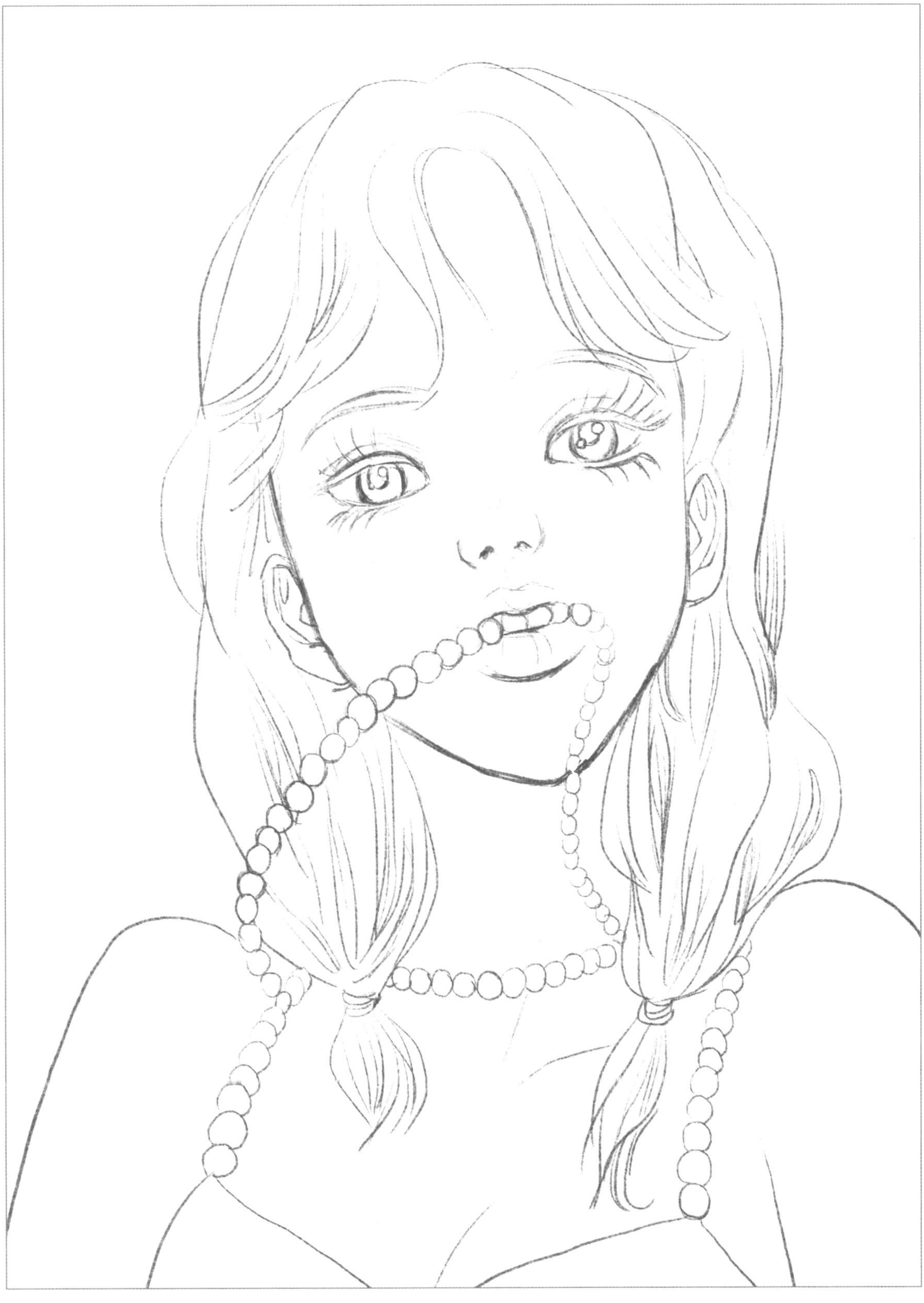

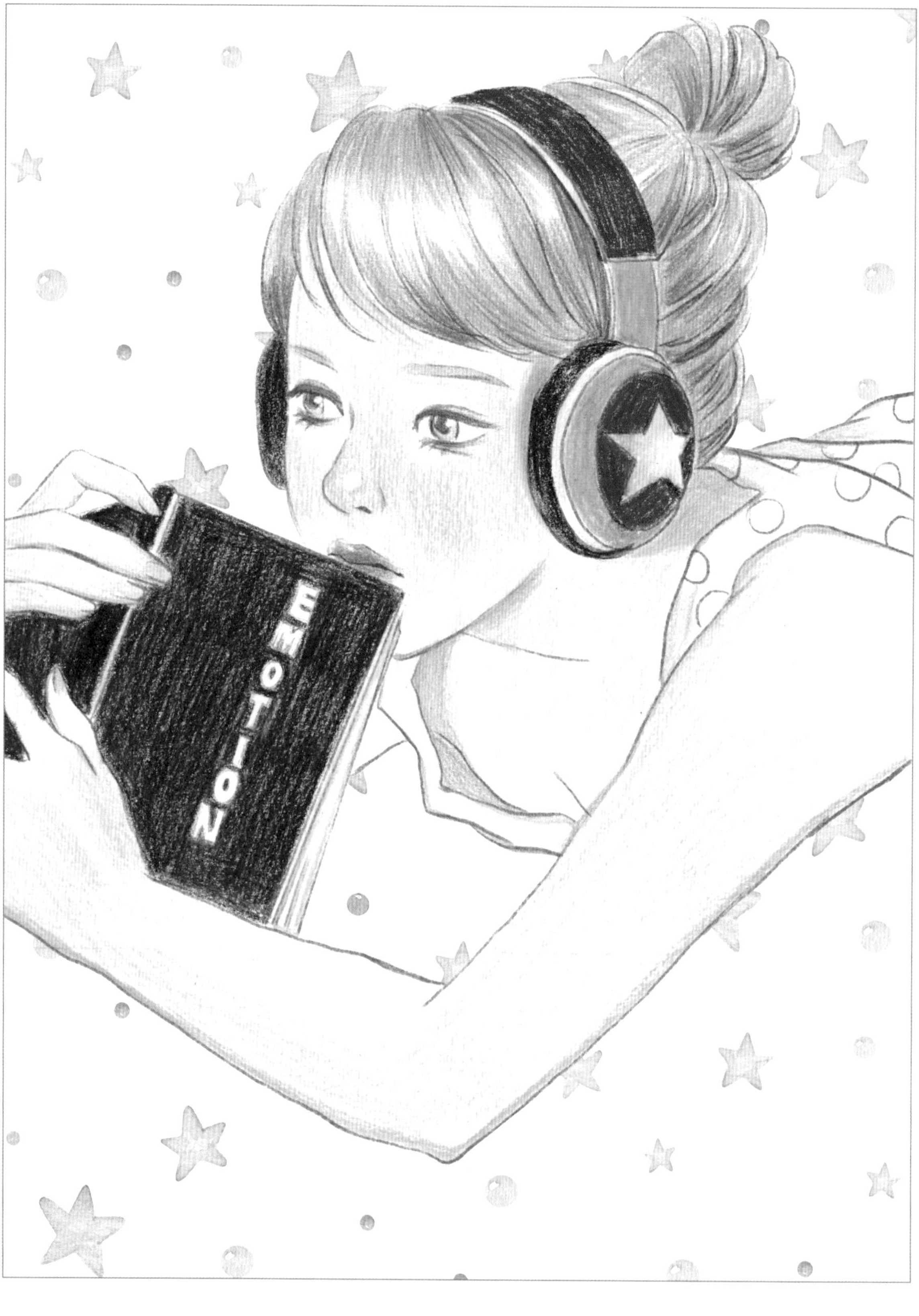
EMOTION

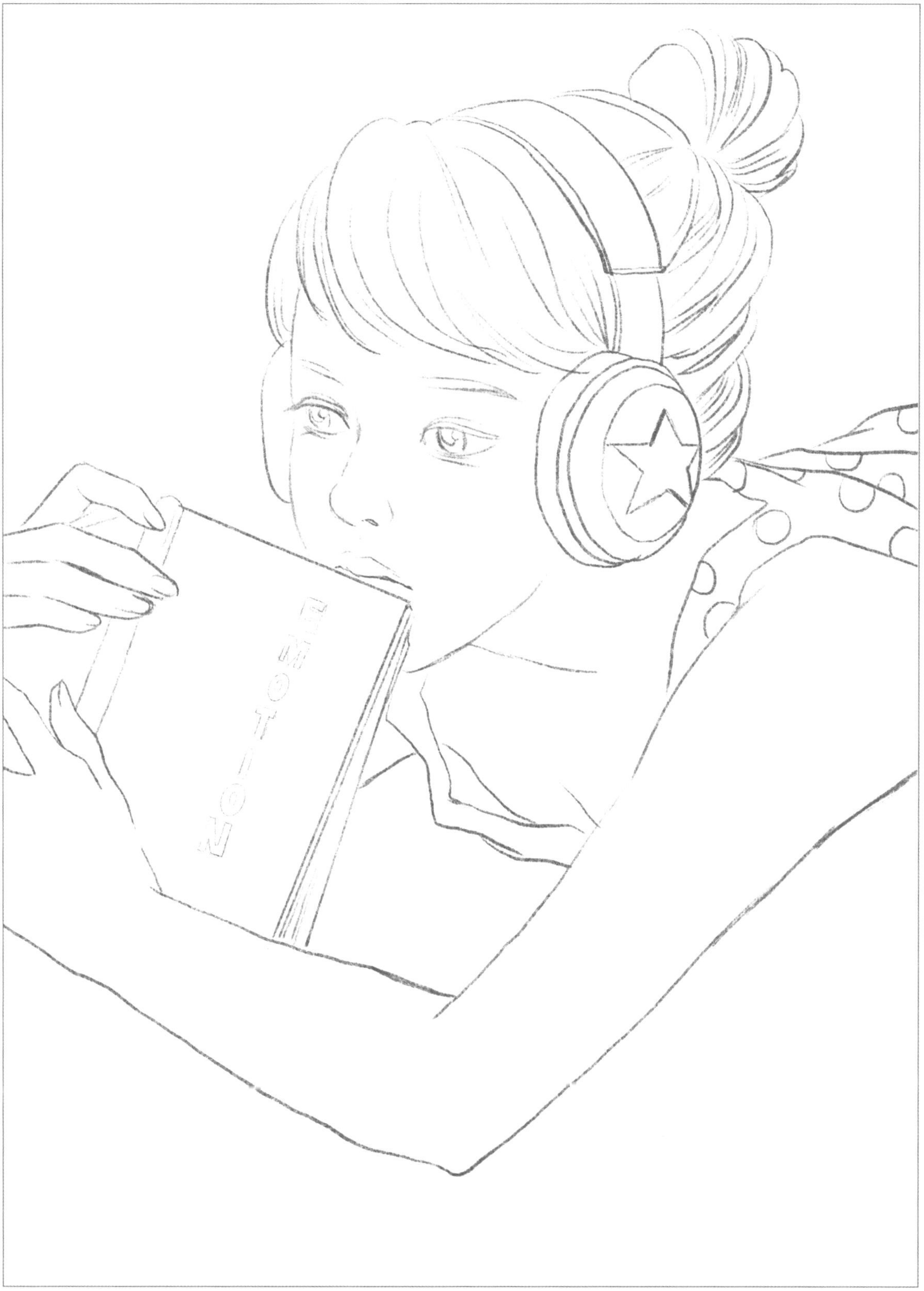
EMOTION

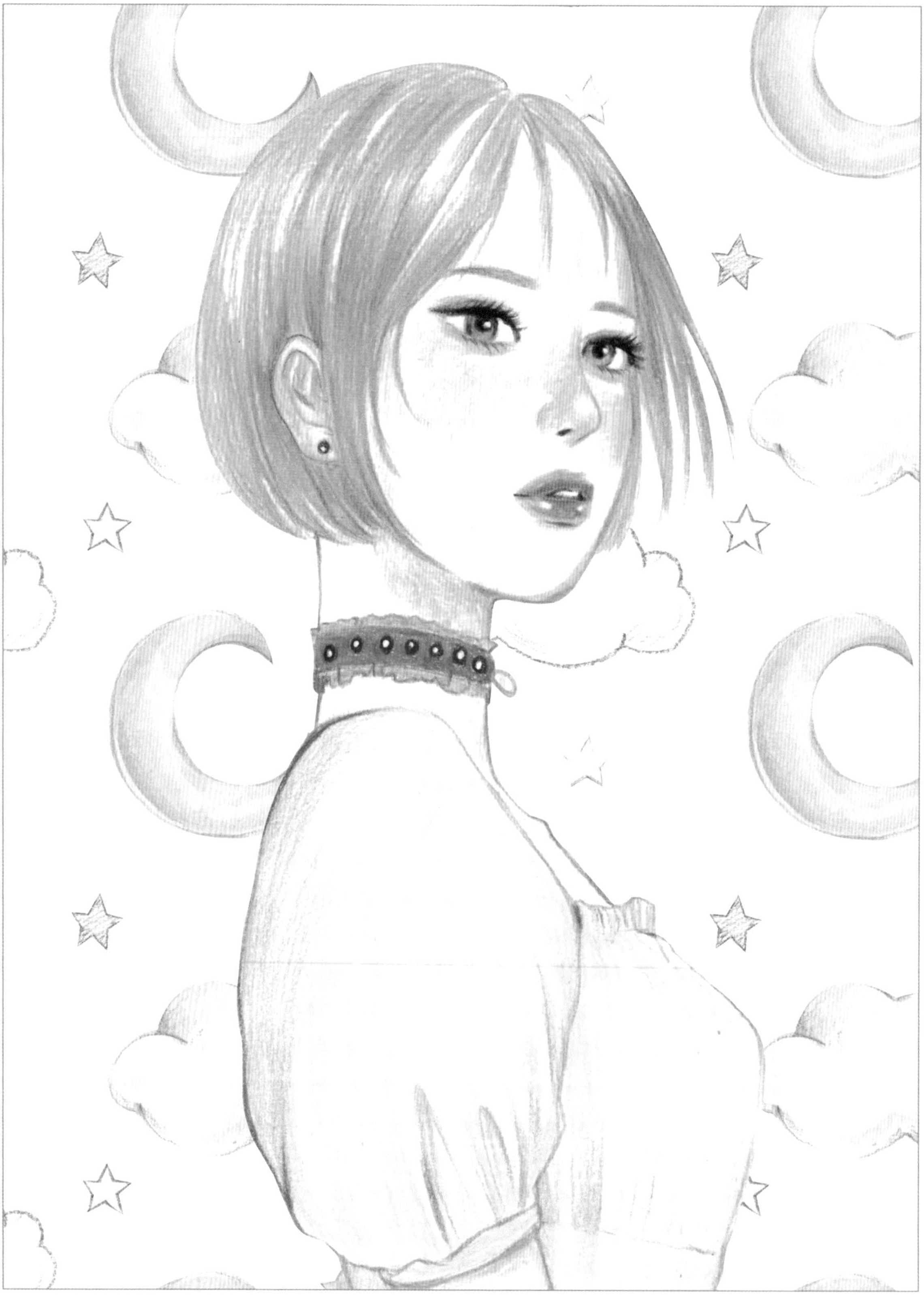

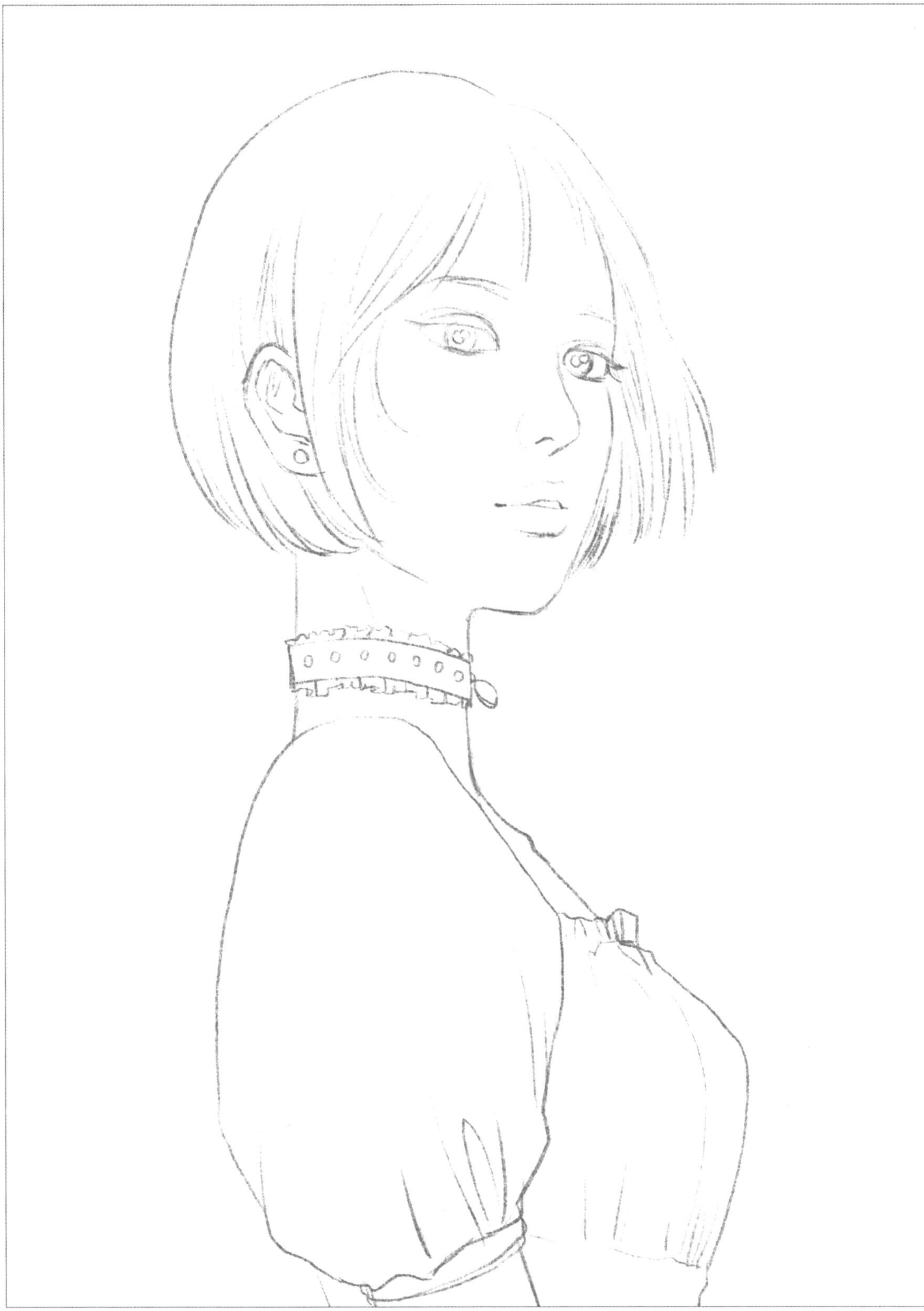

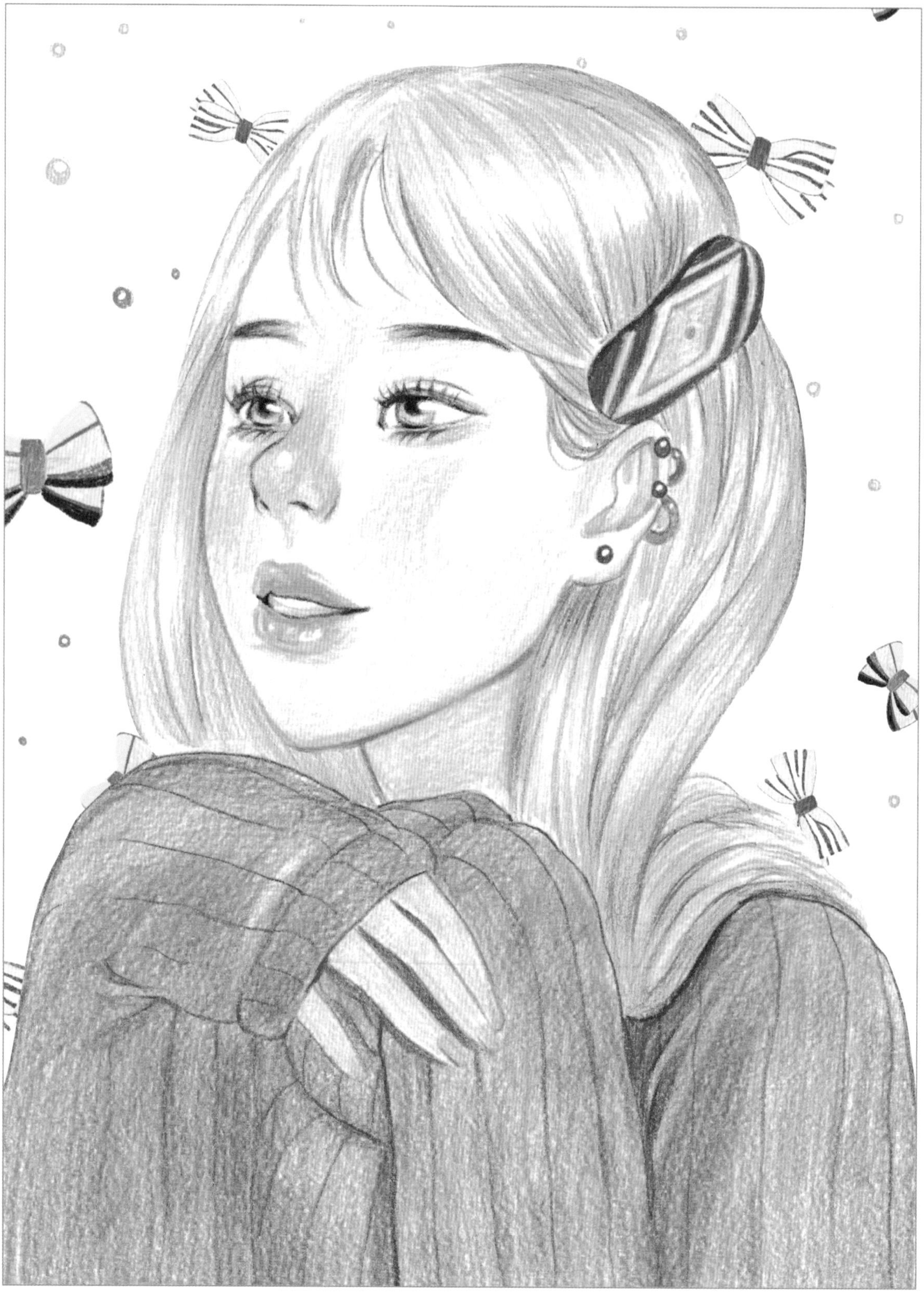

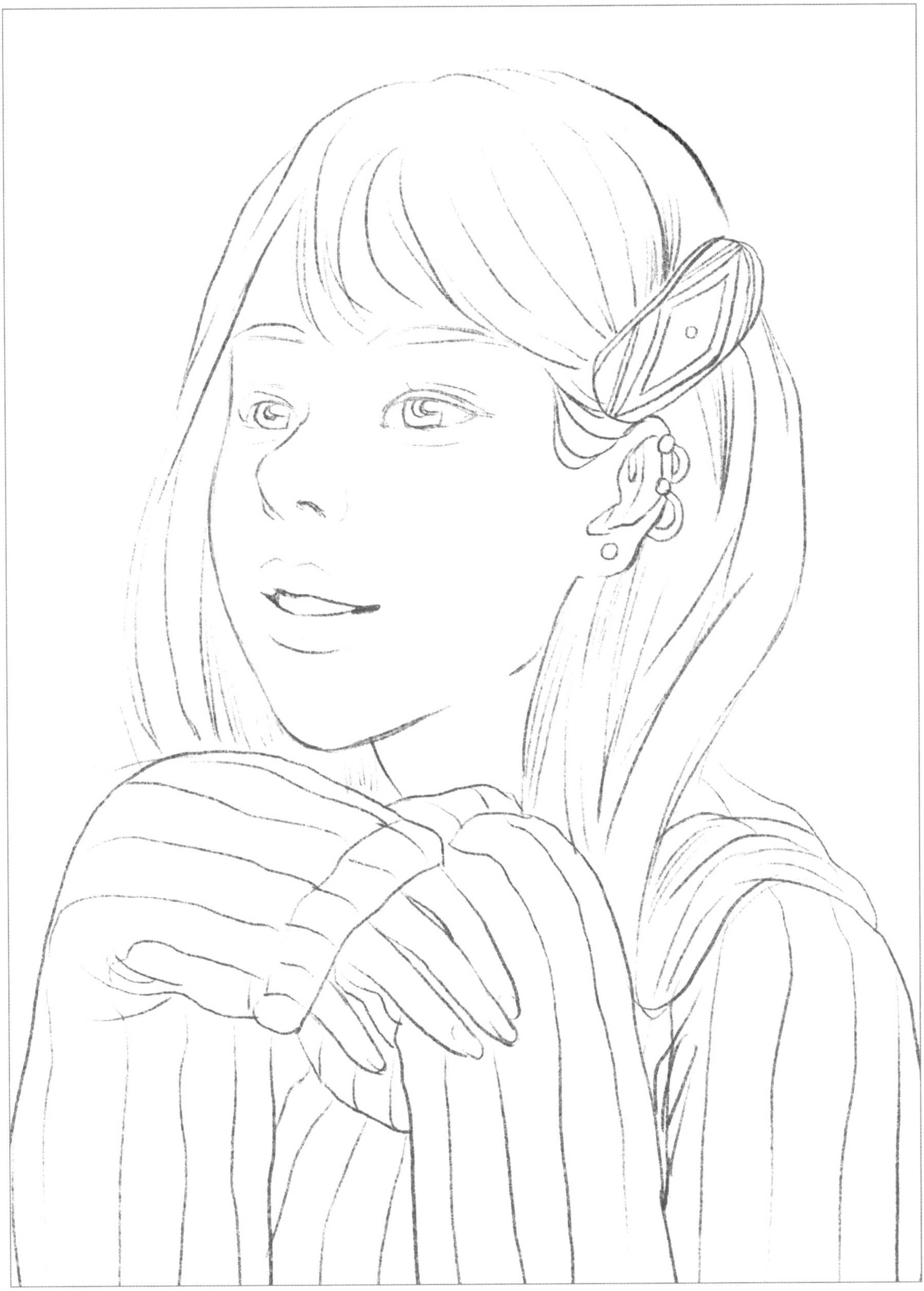

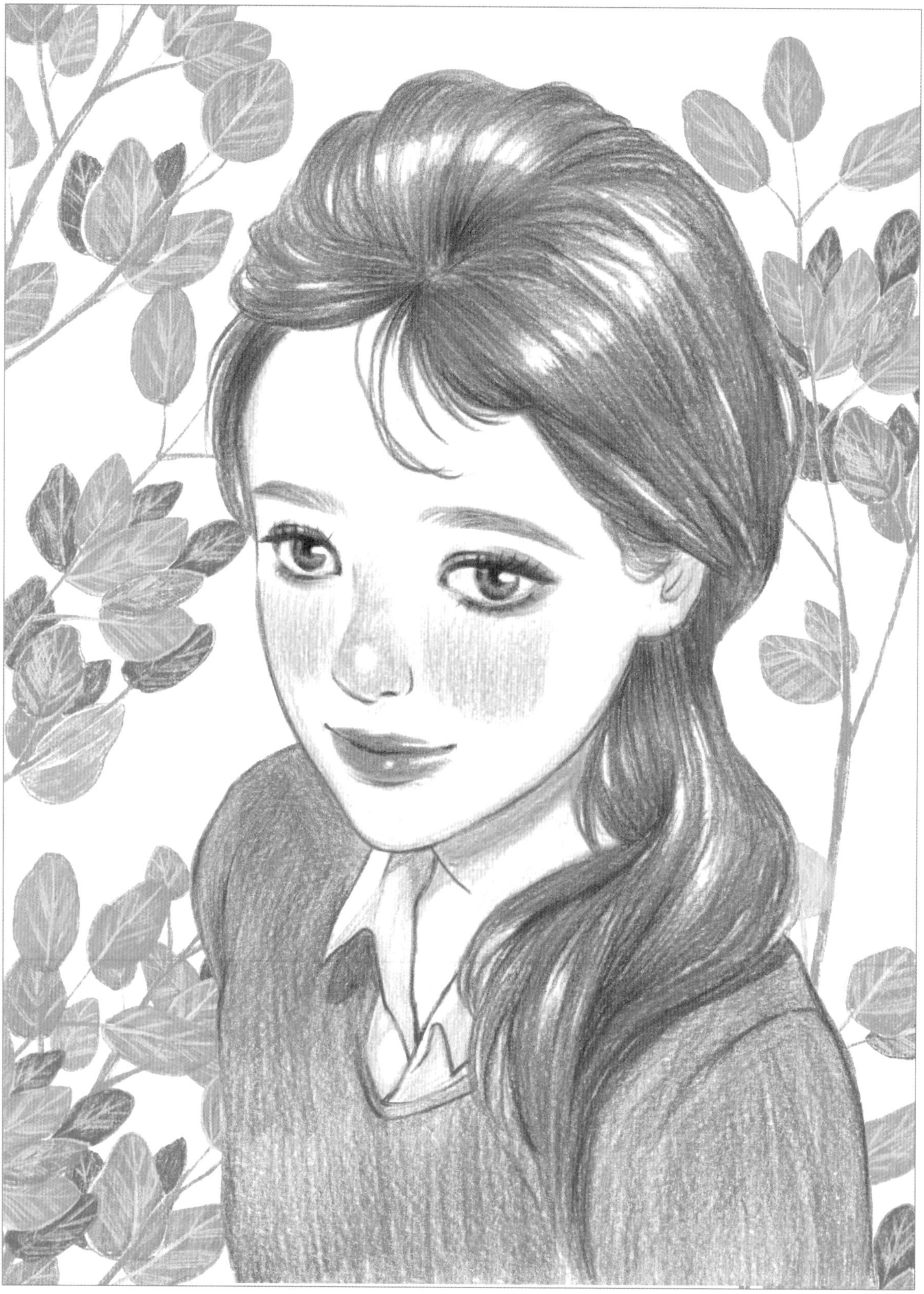

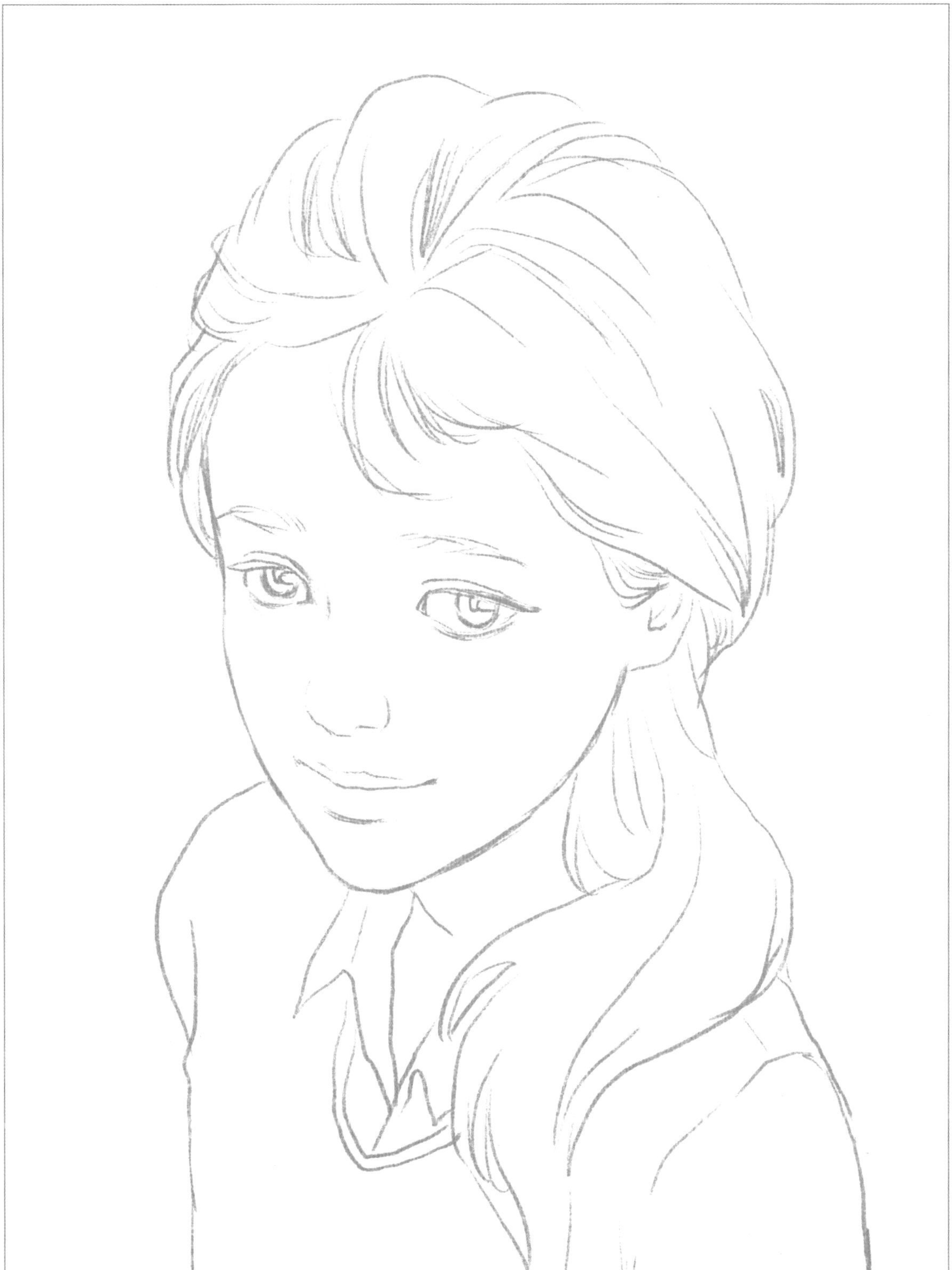

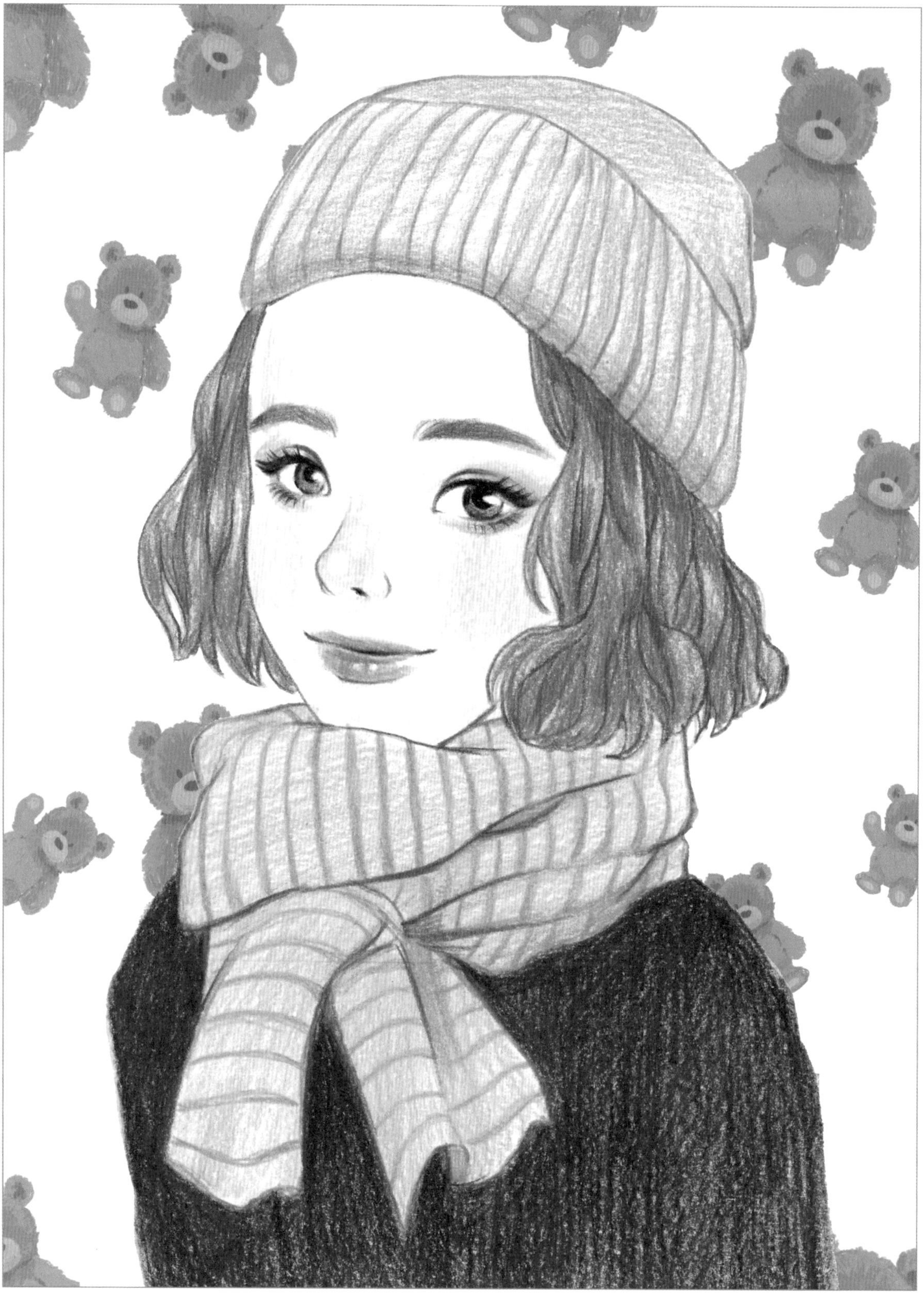

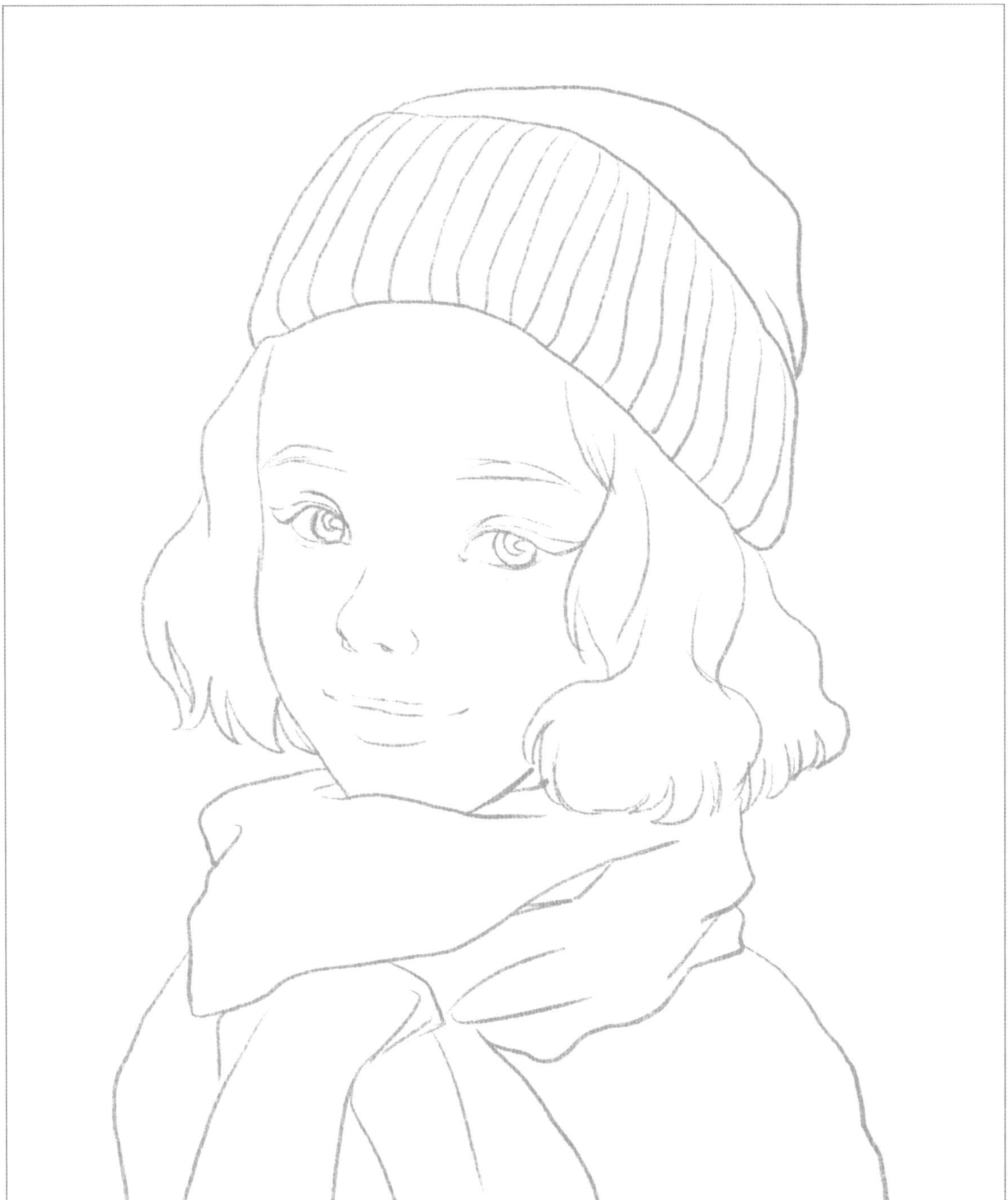

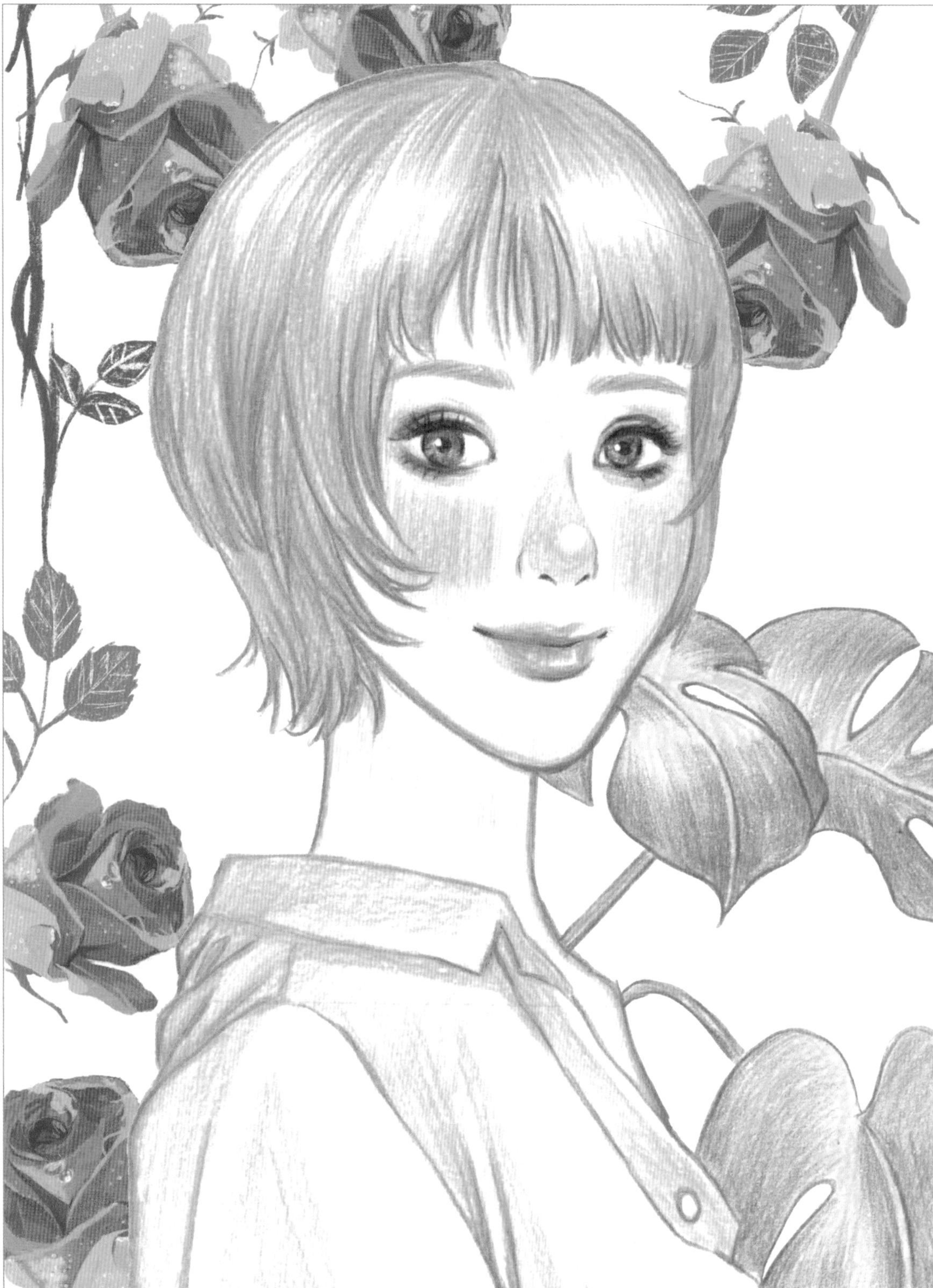

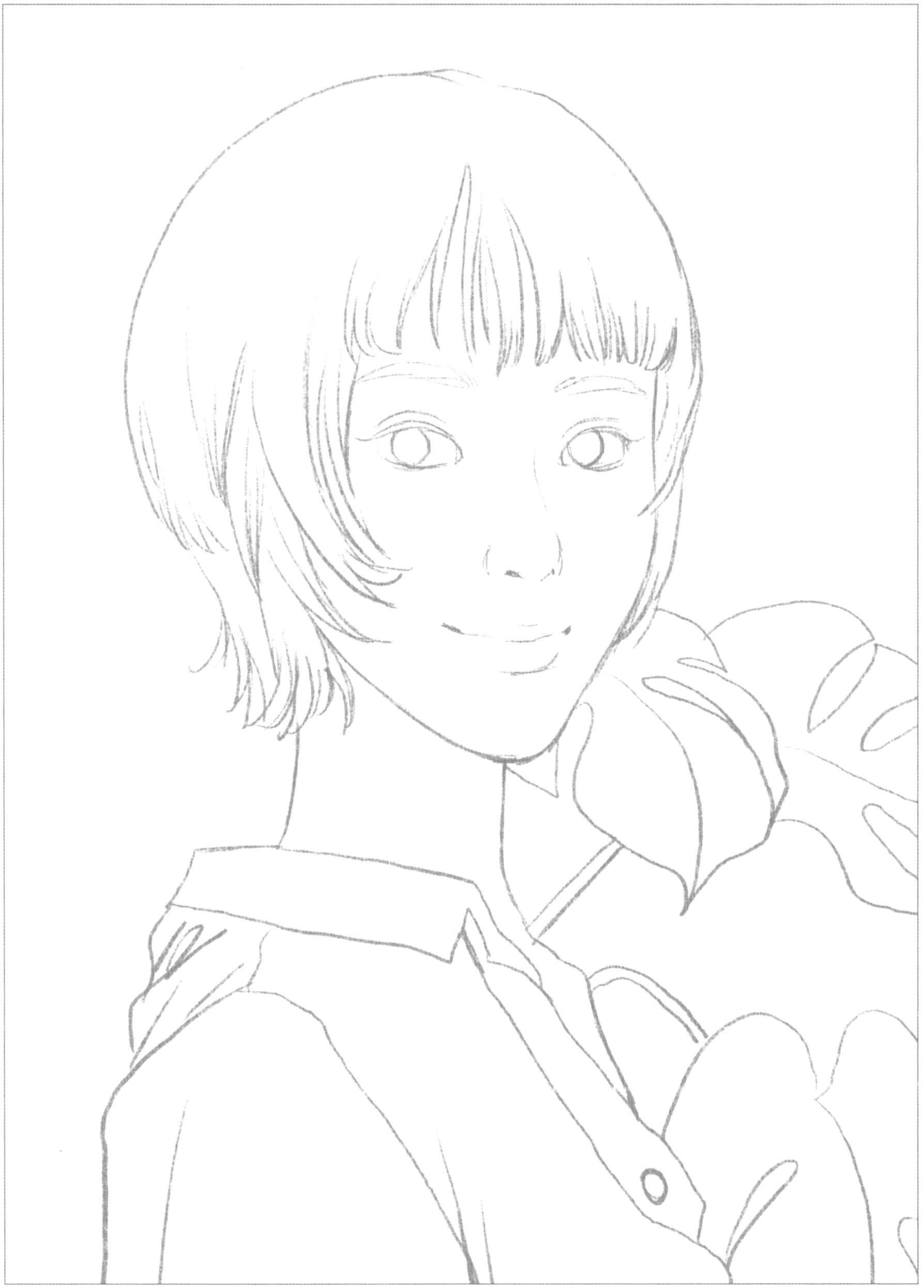

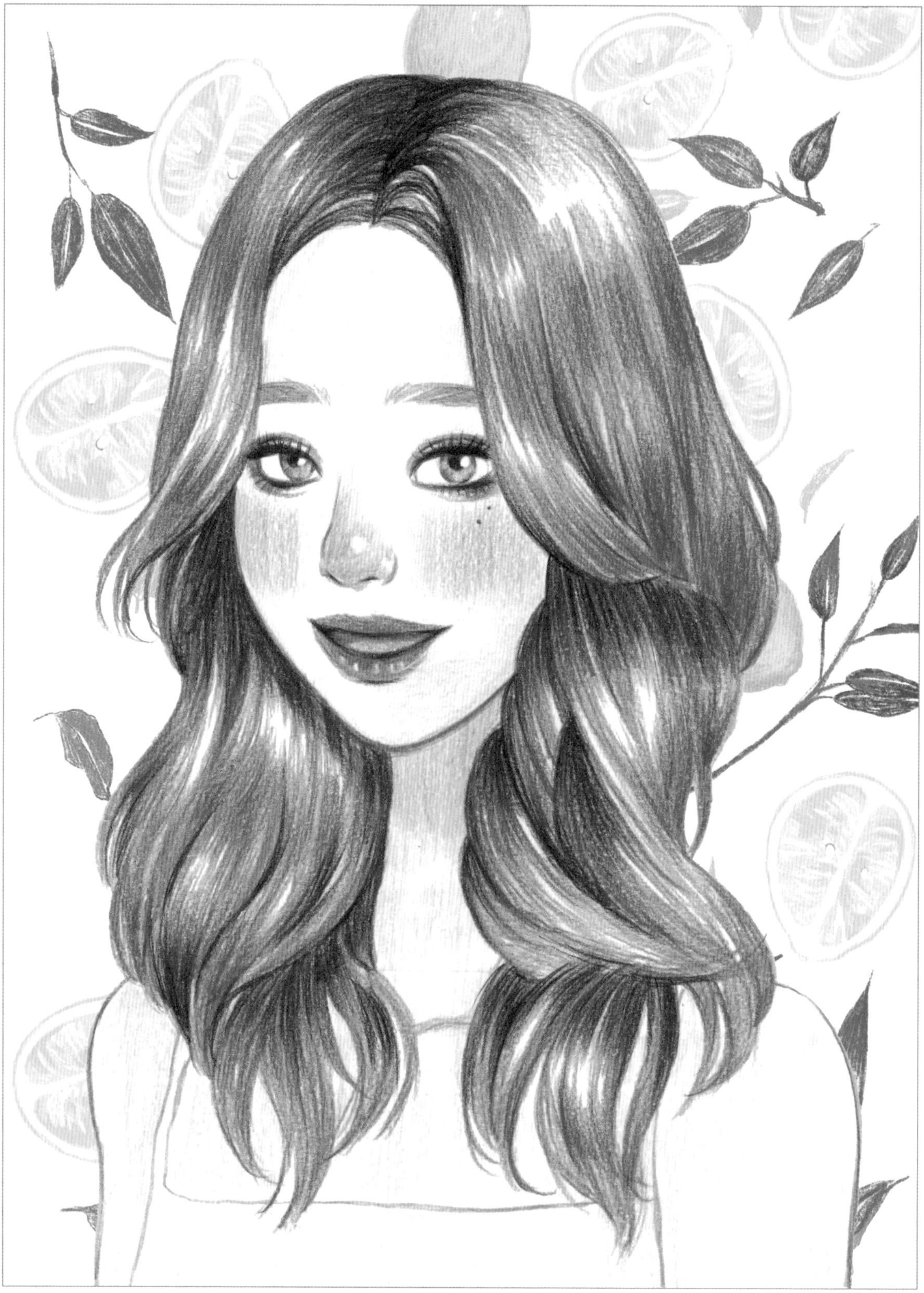

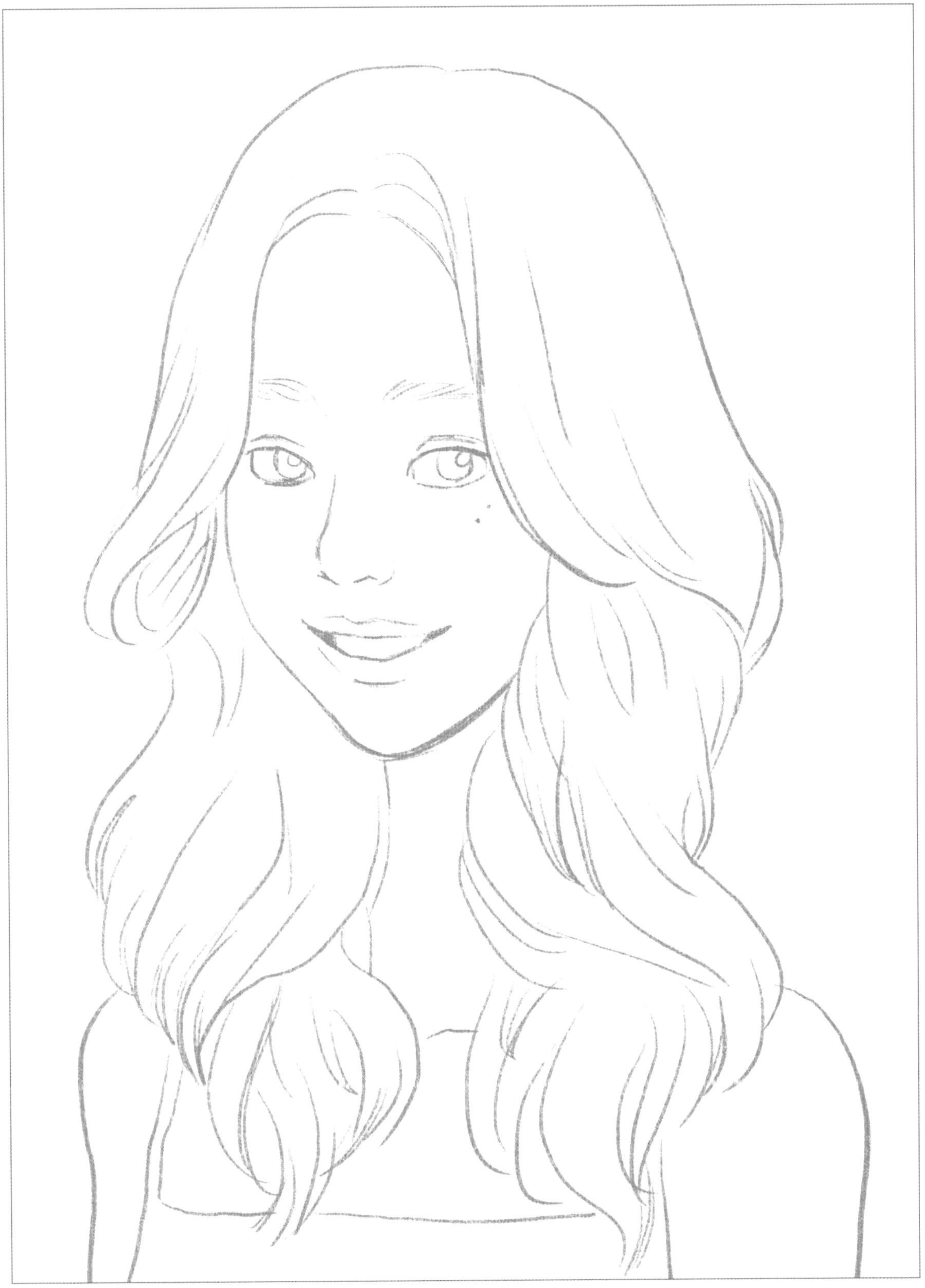

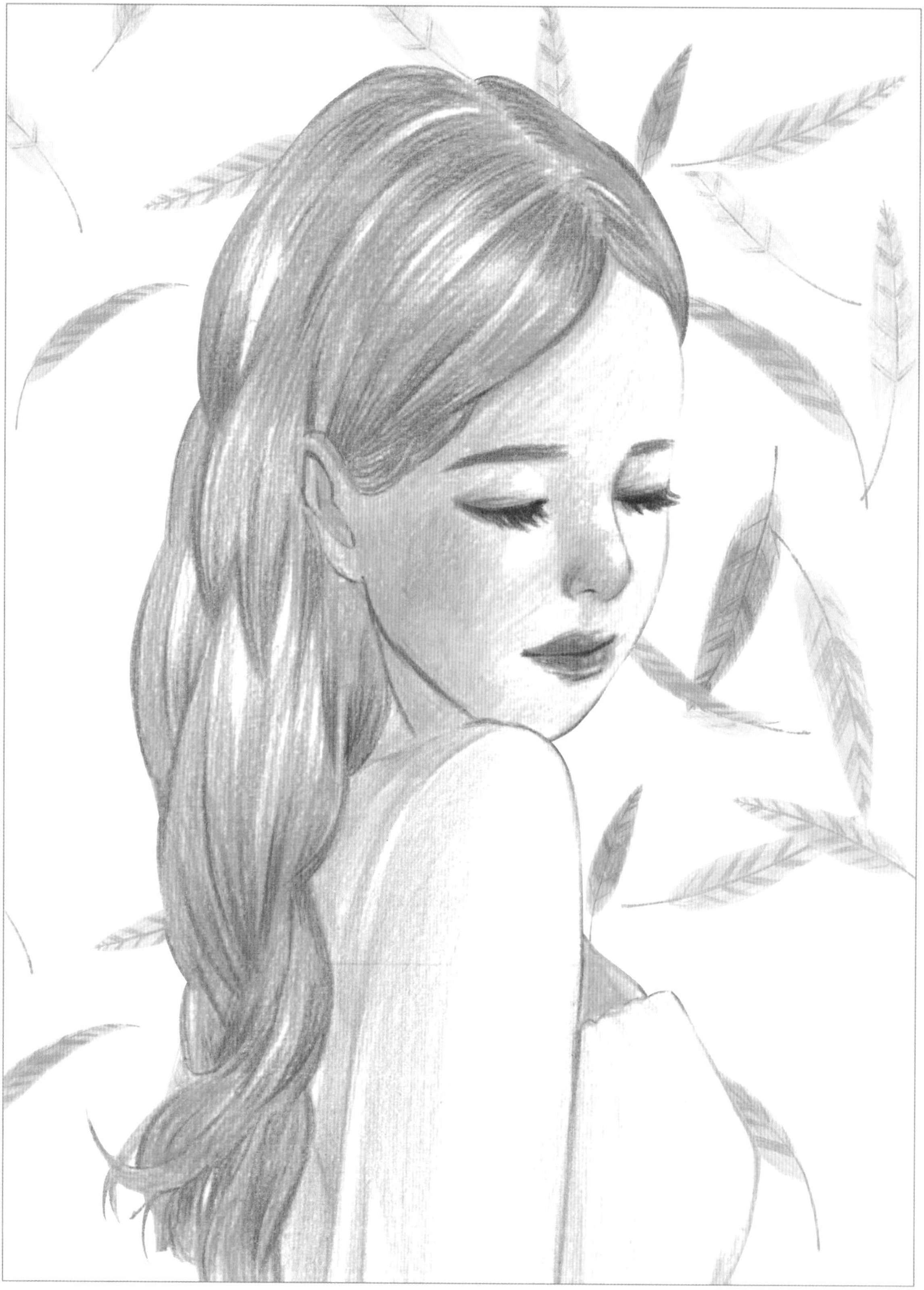

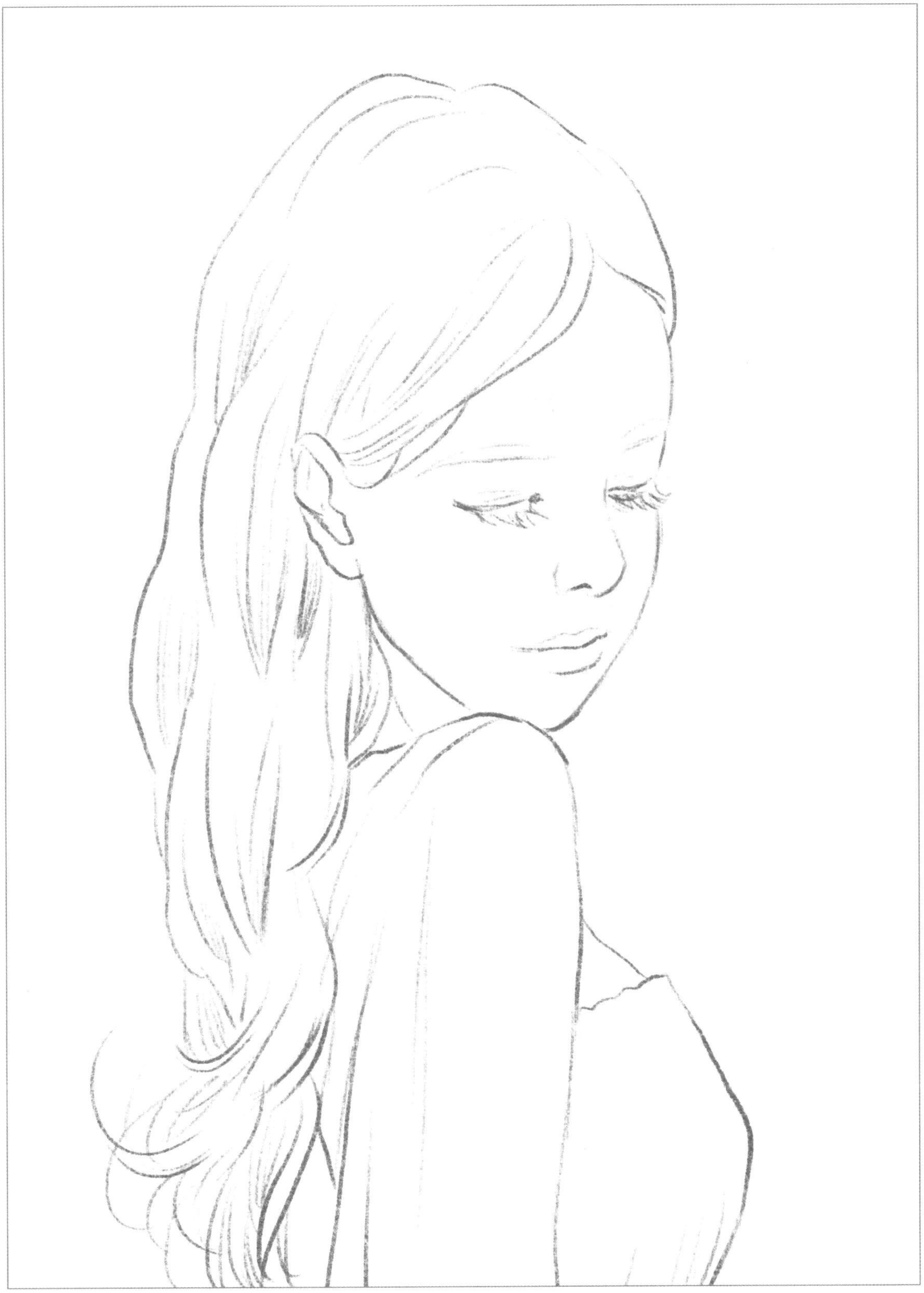

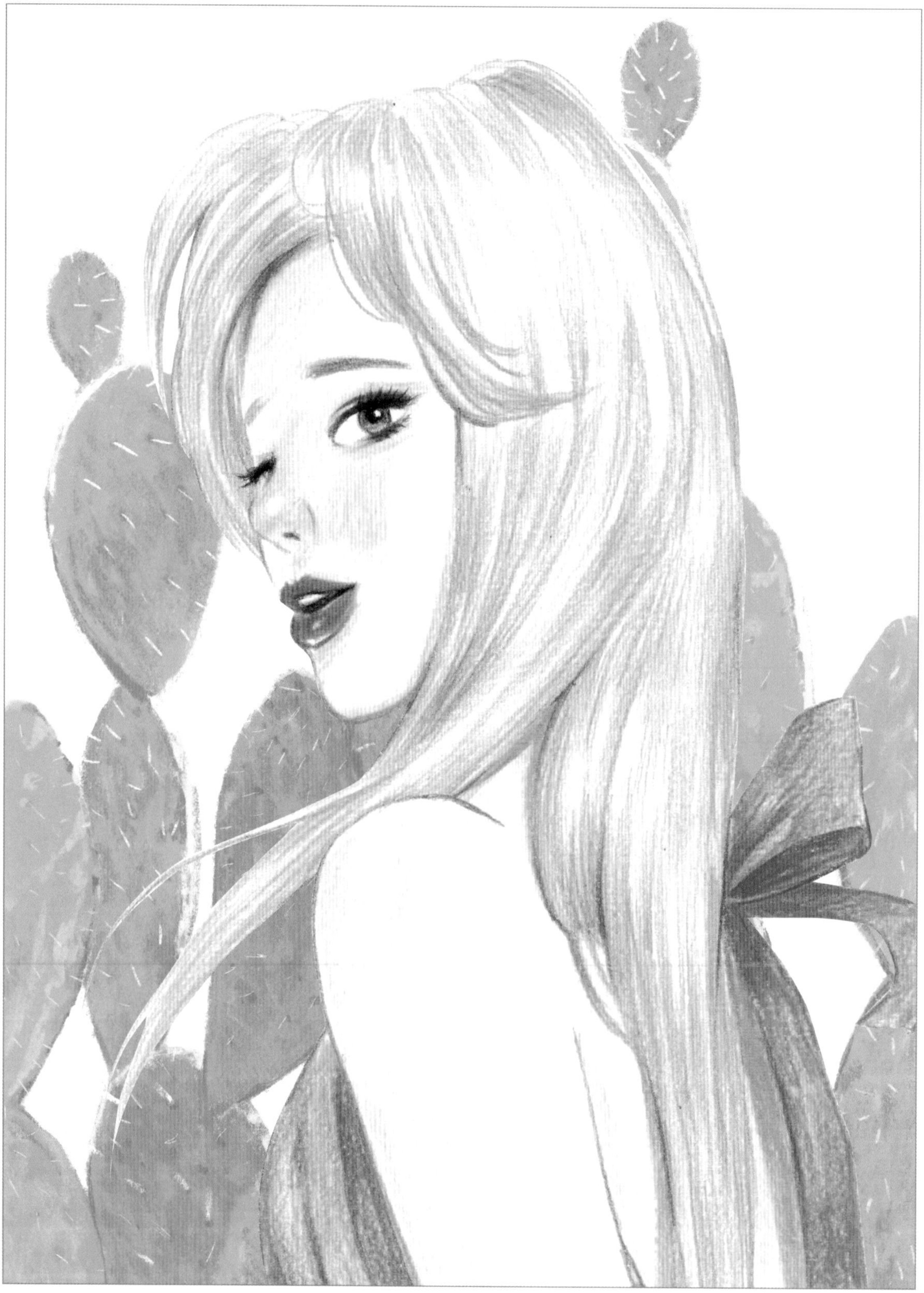

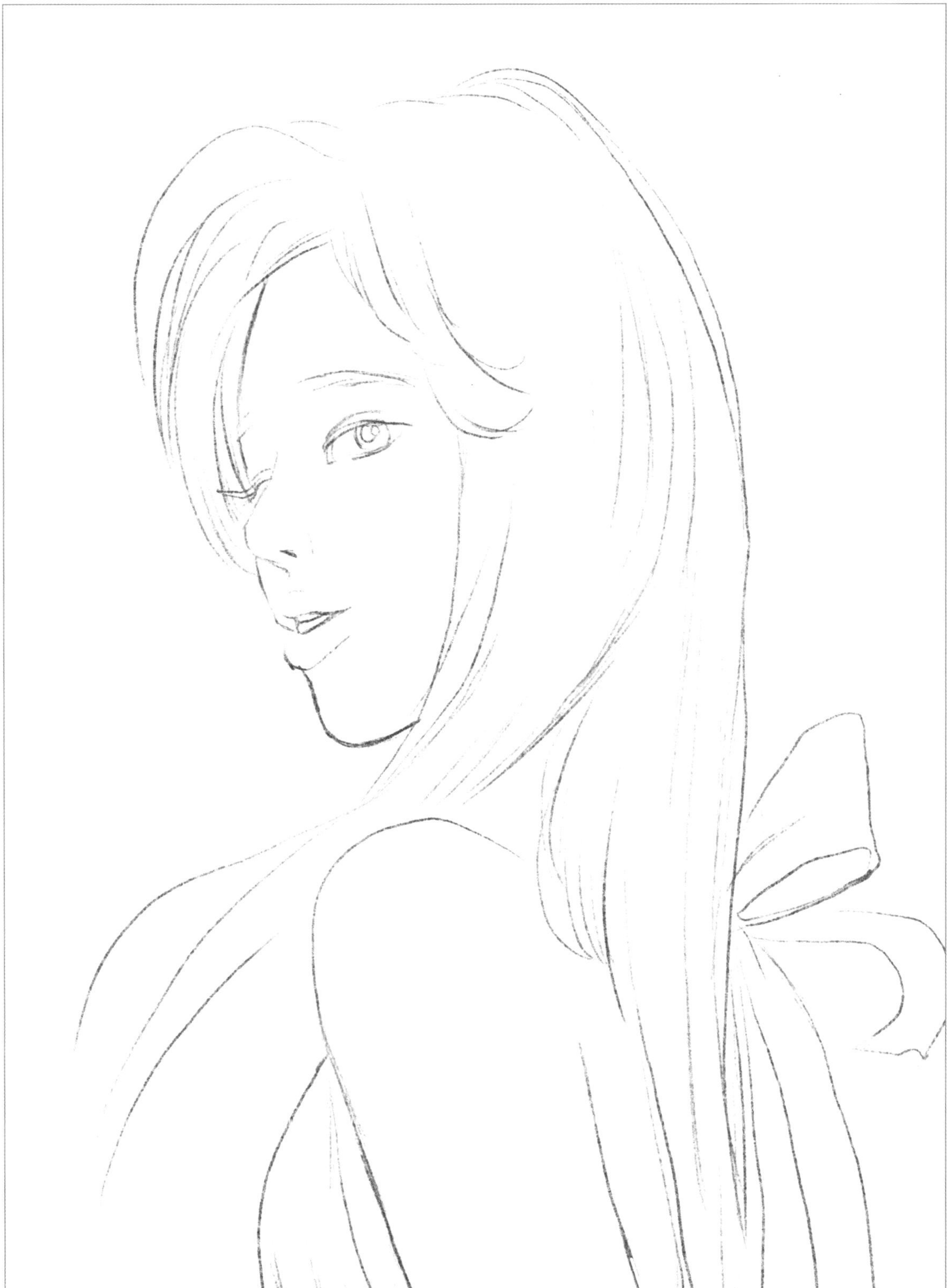

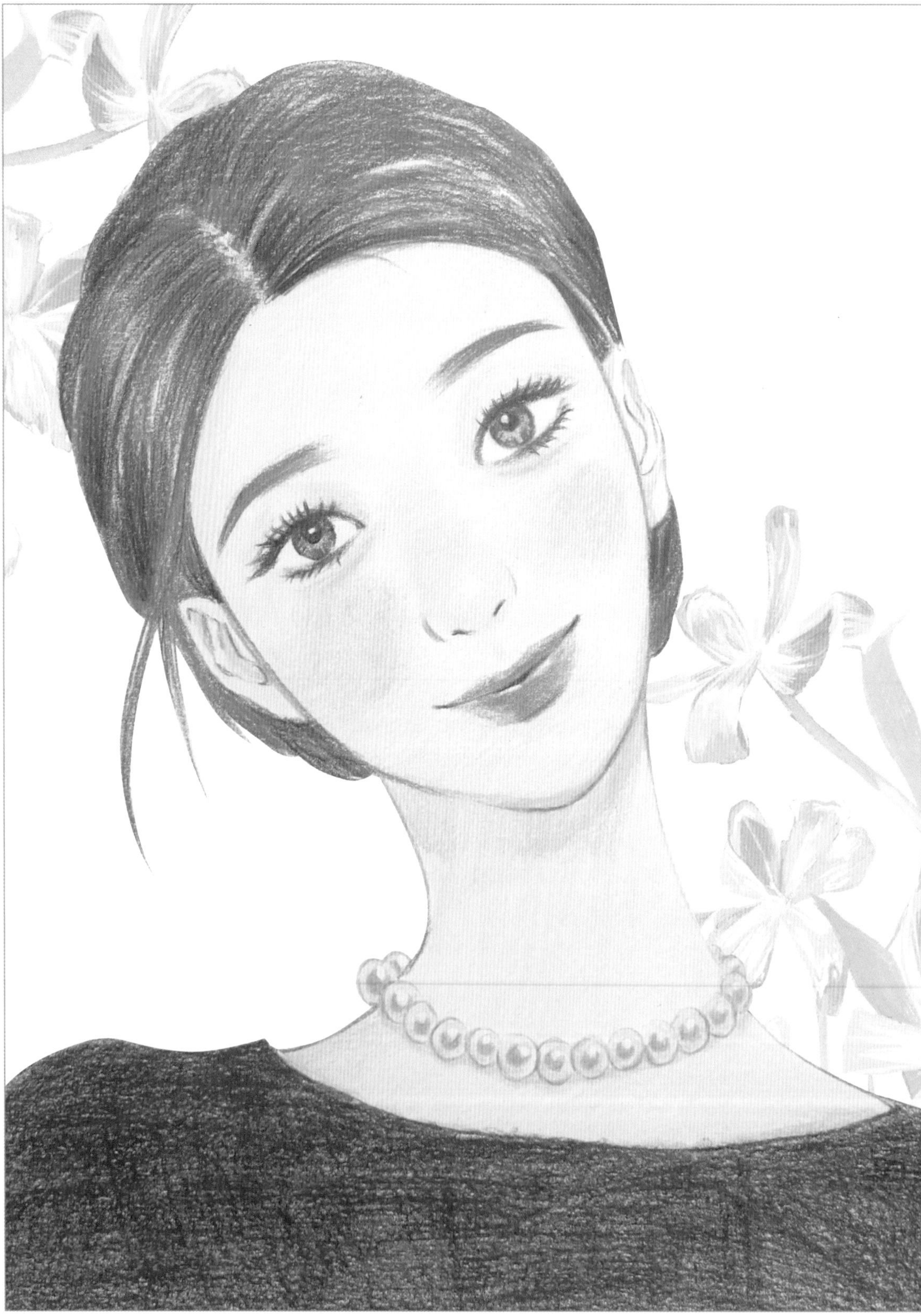

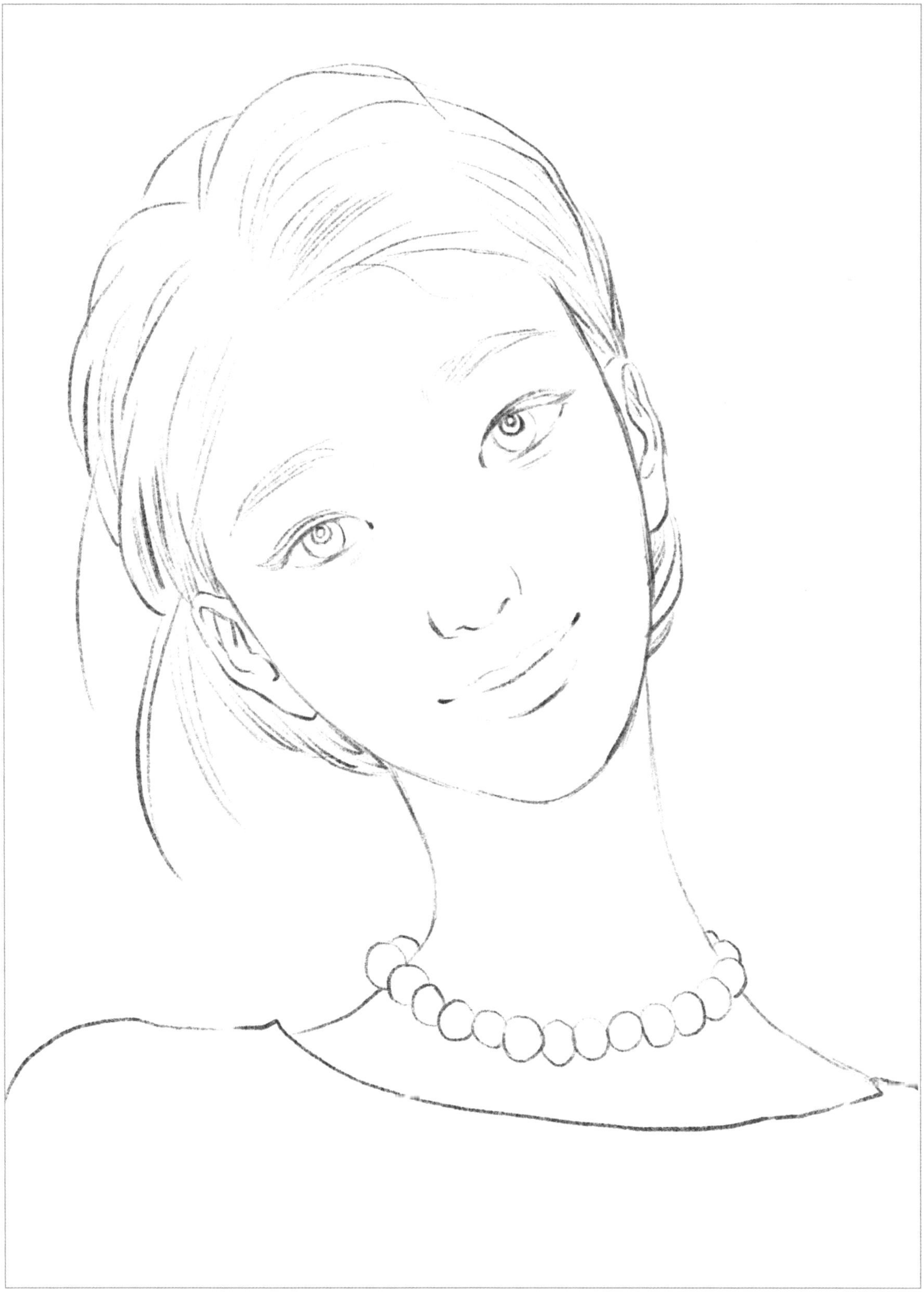

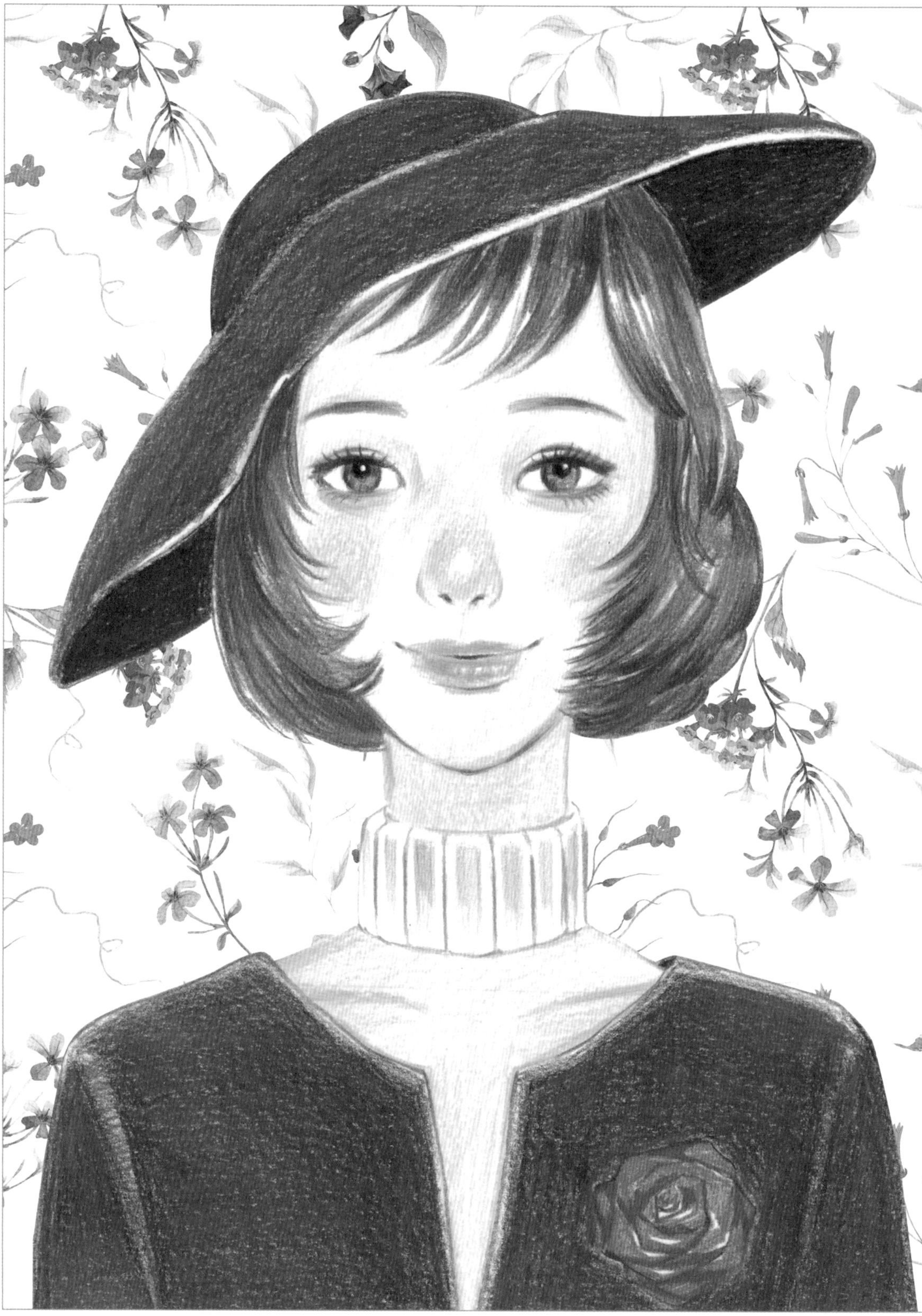

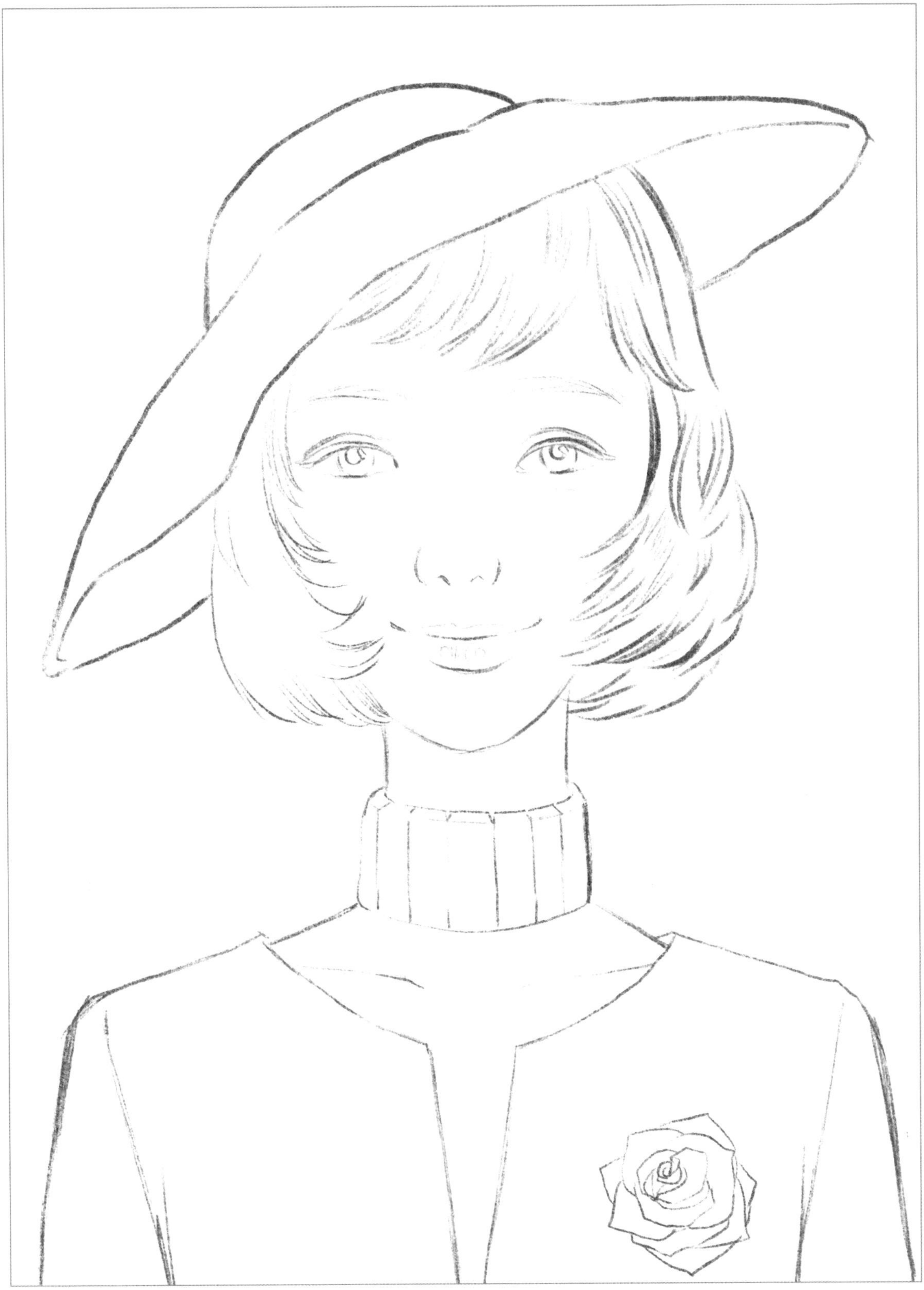

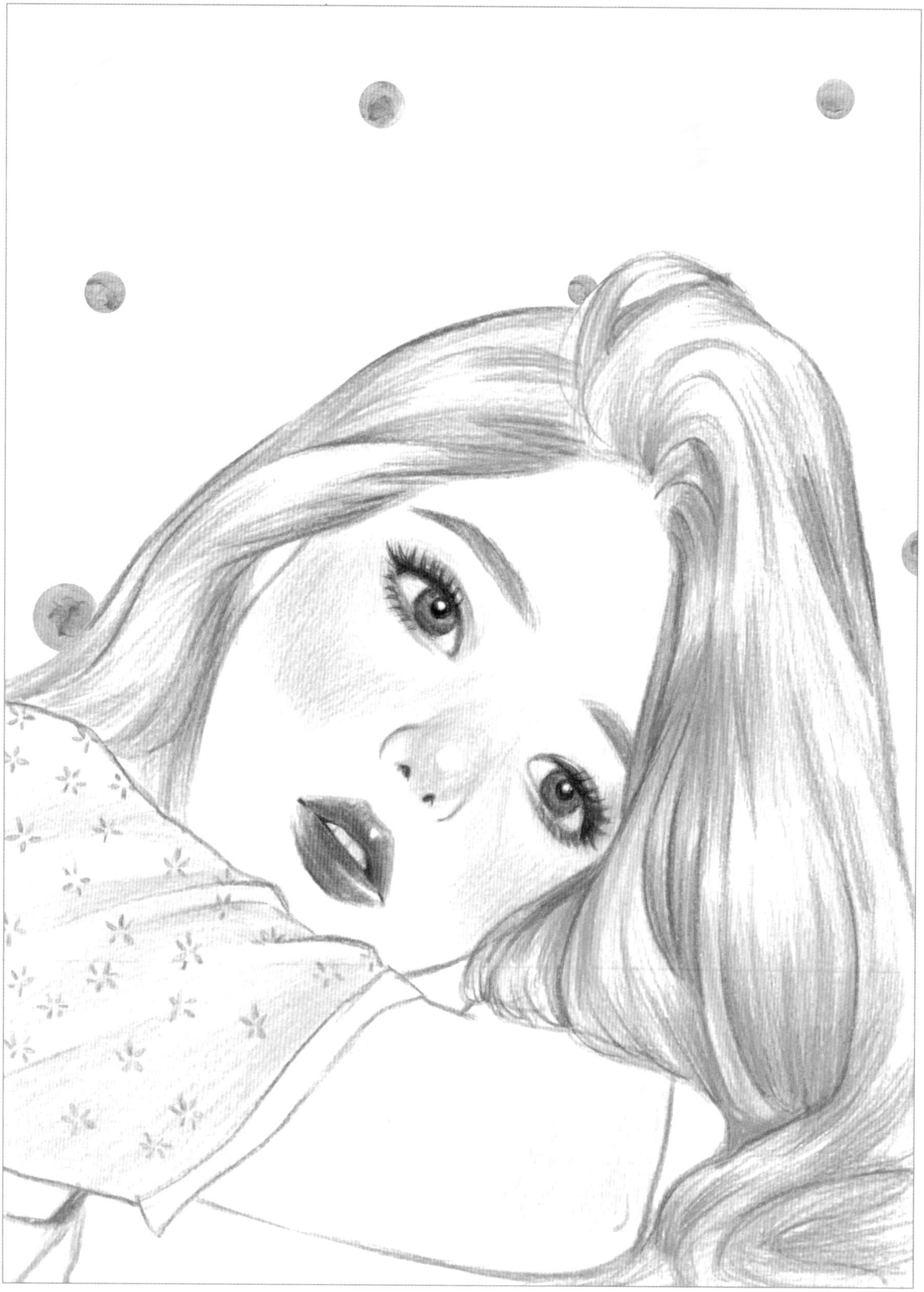

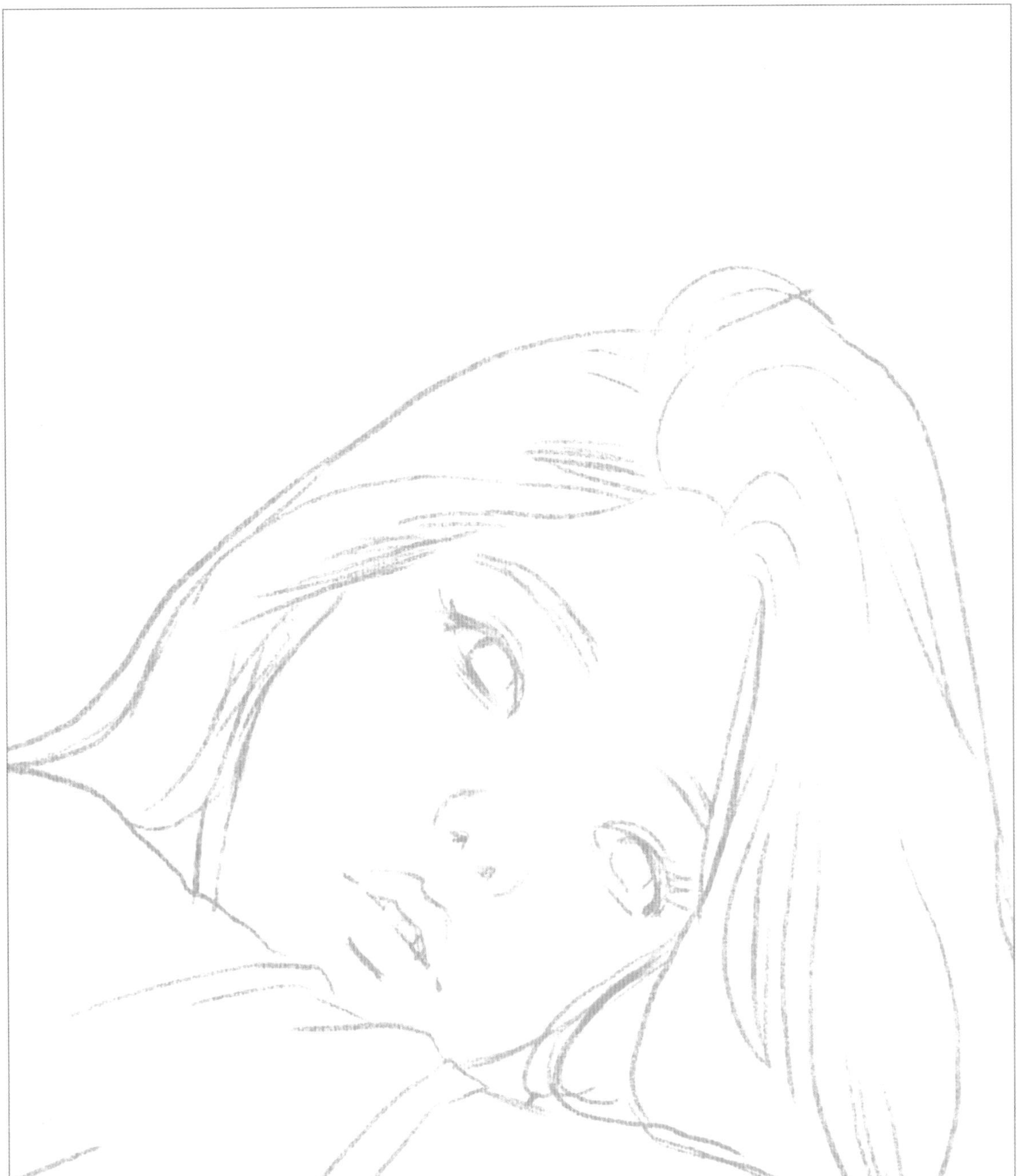

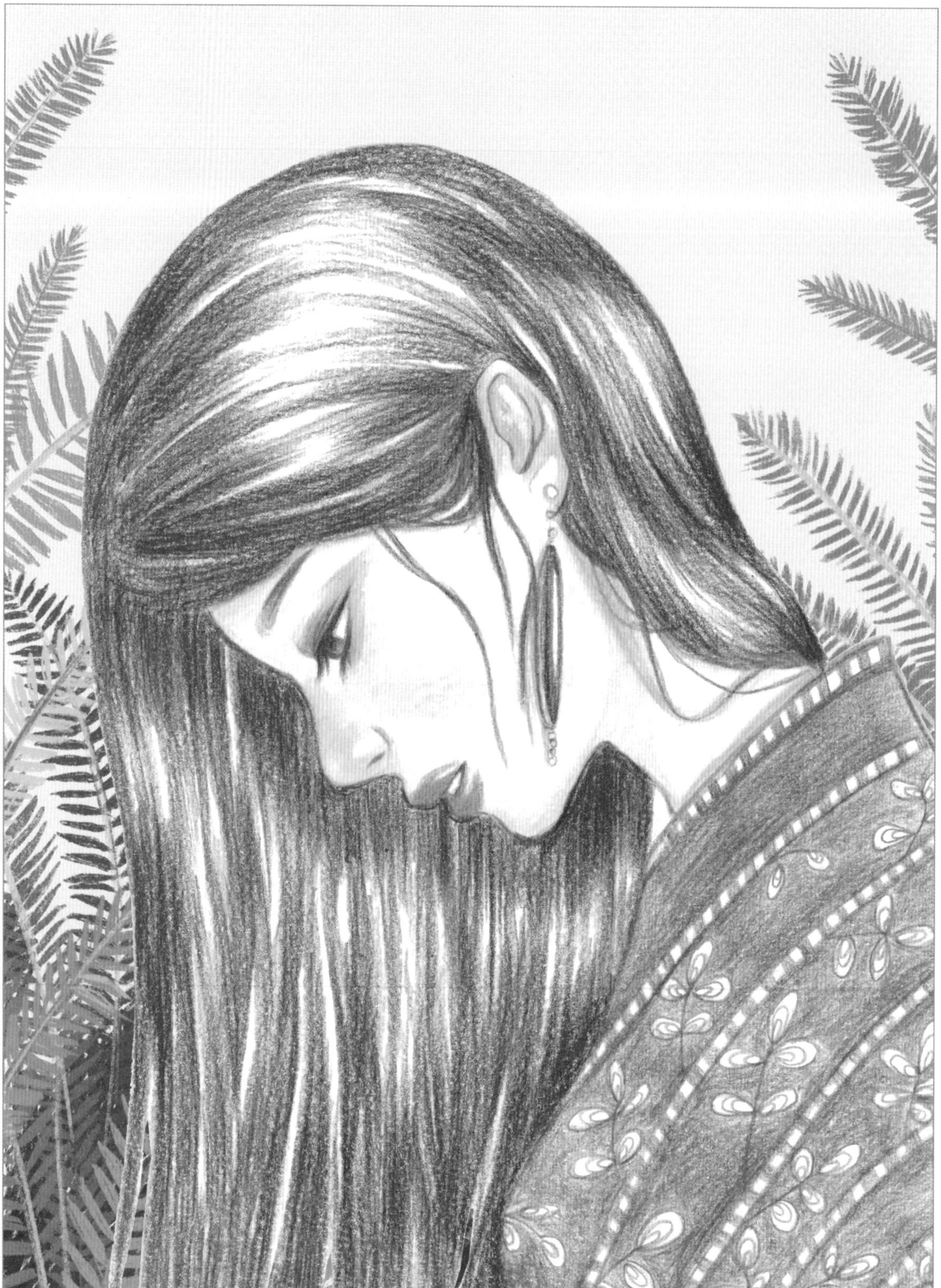

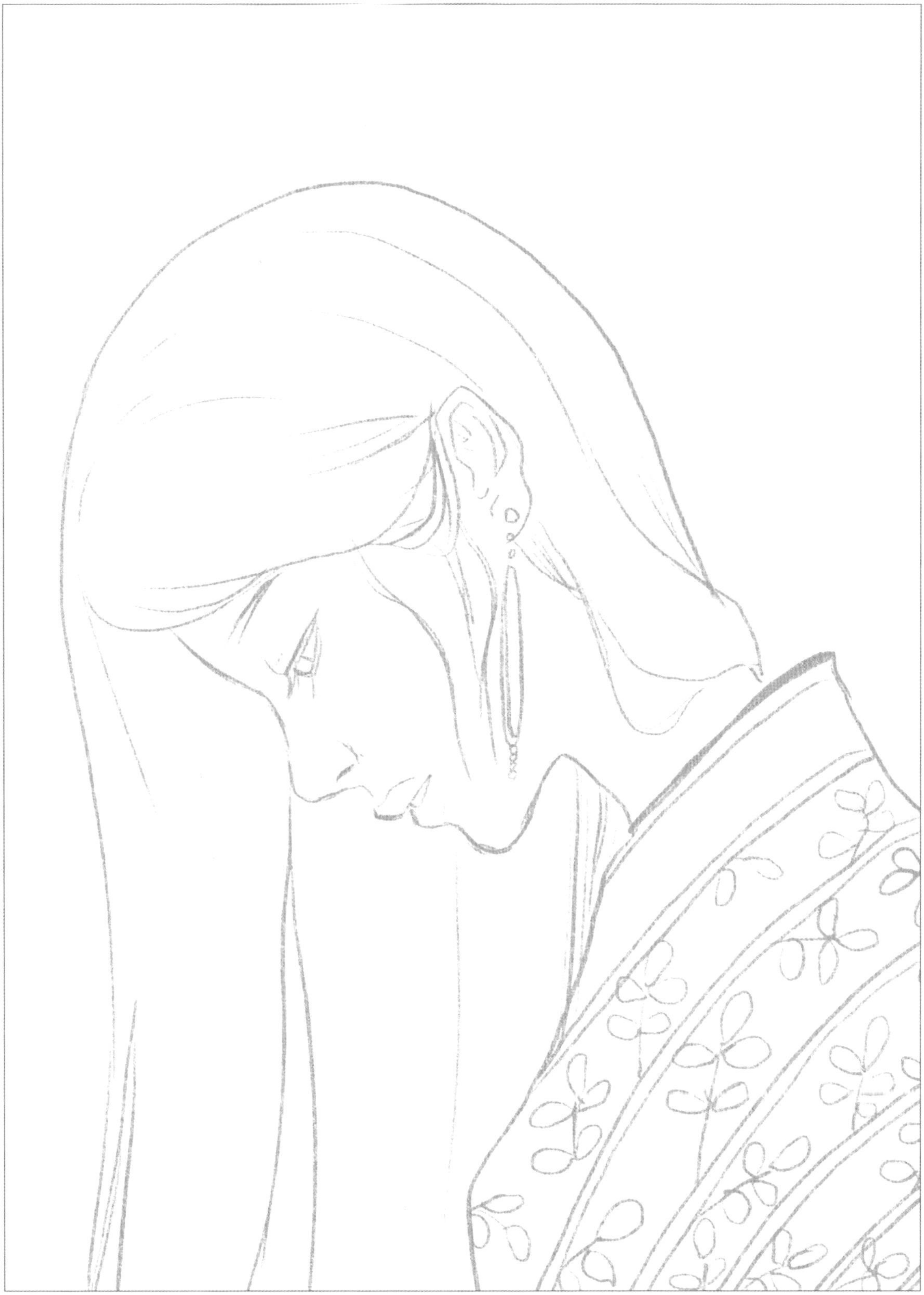

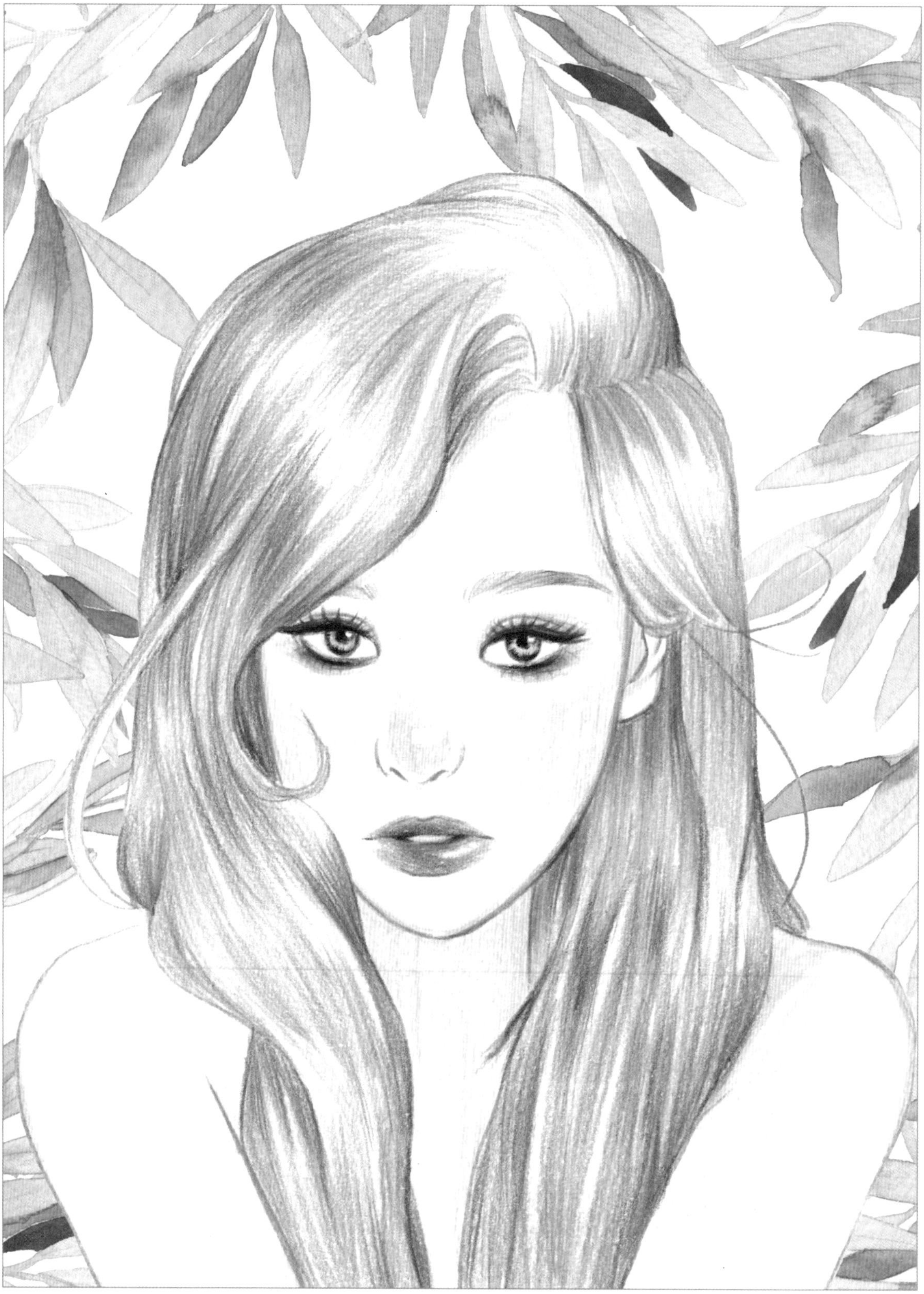

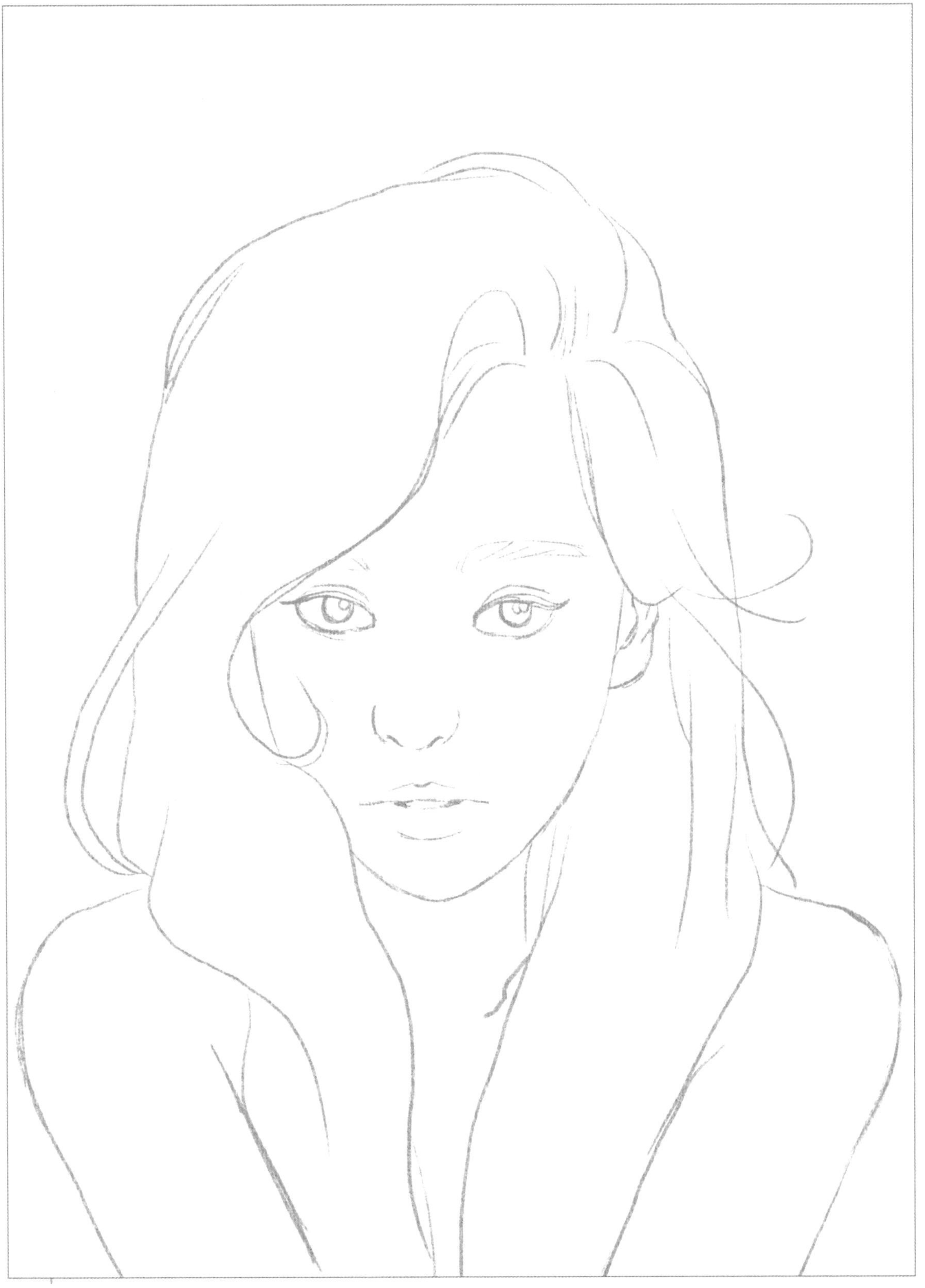

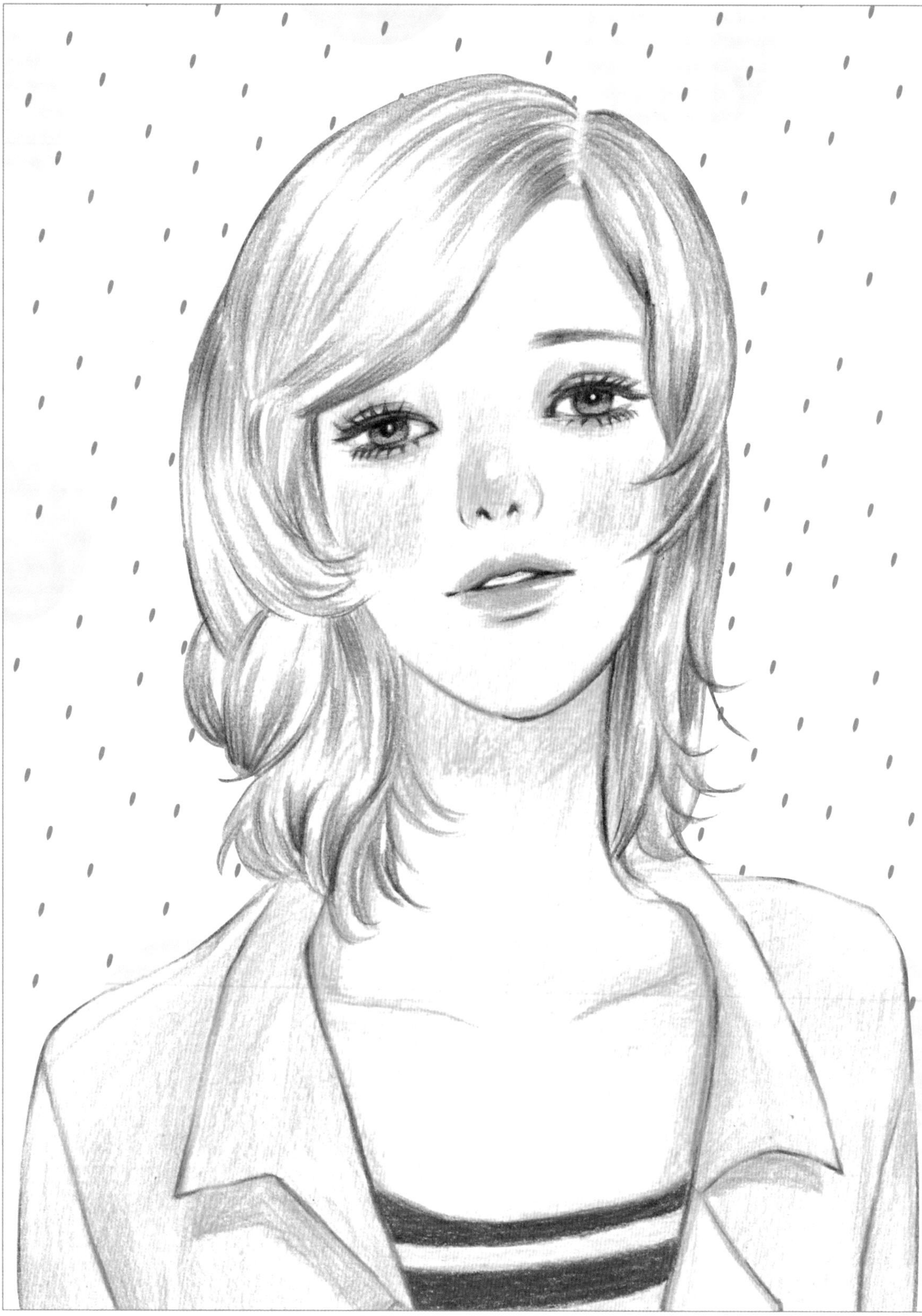

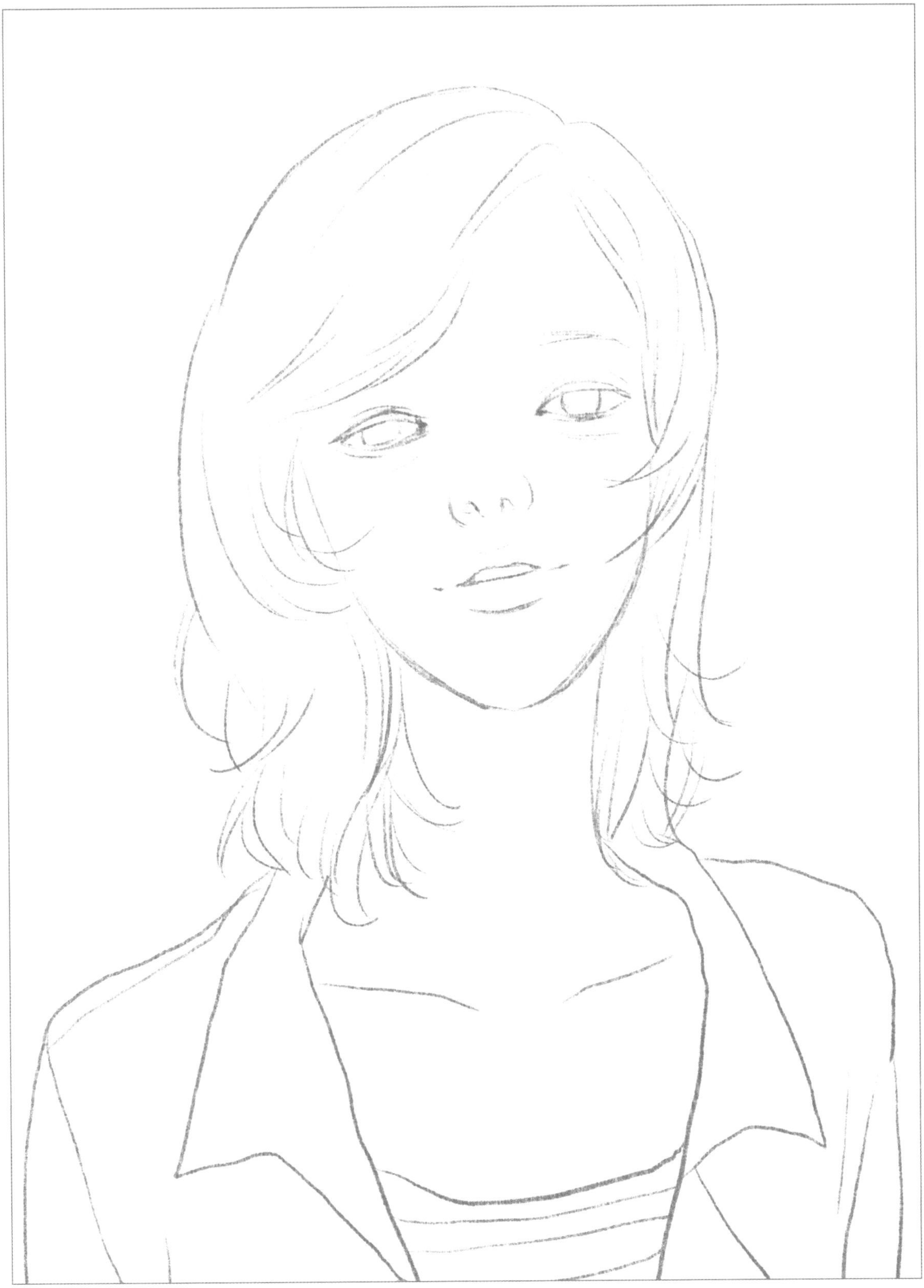

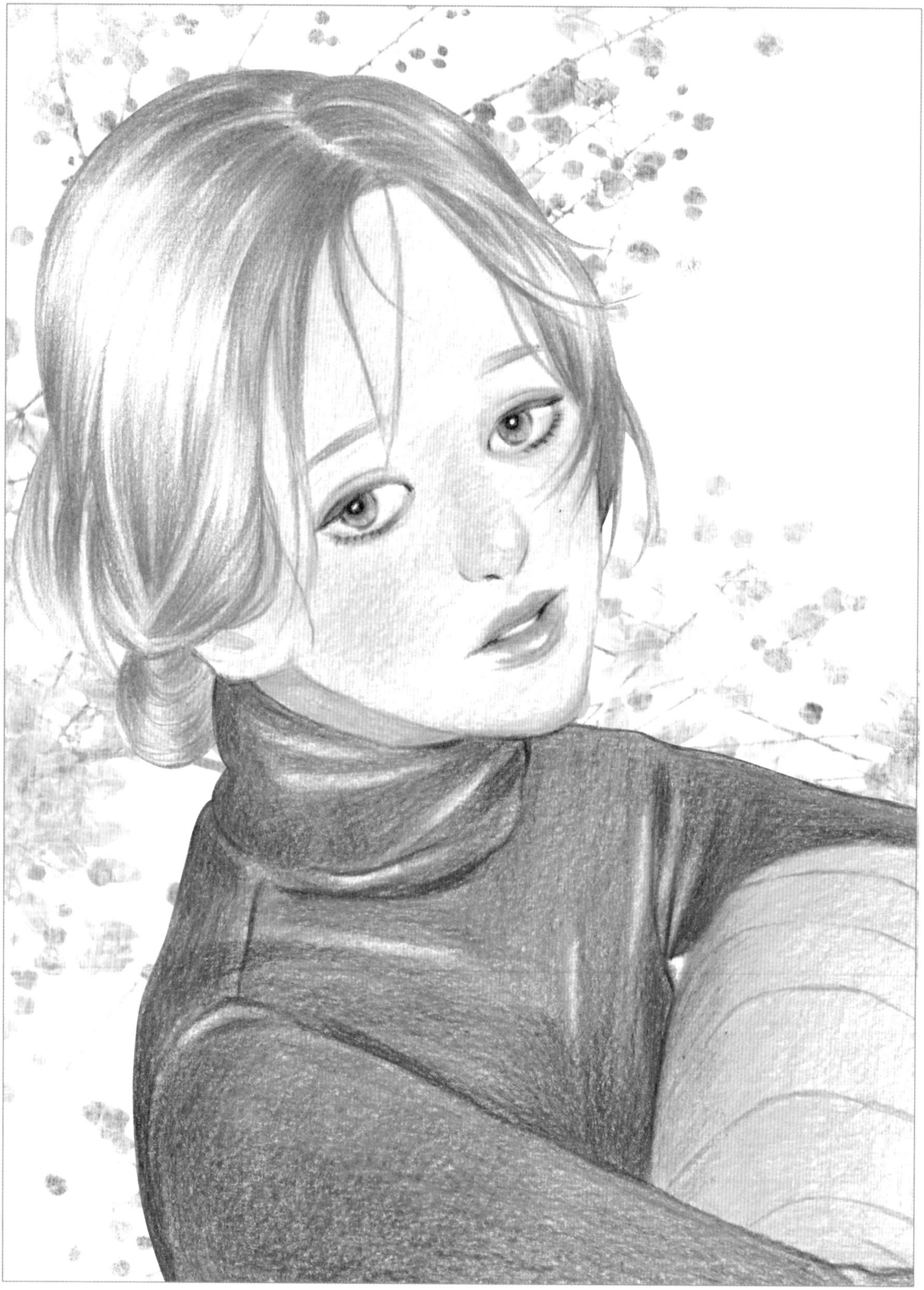

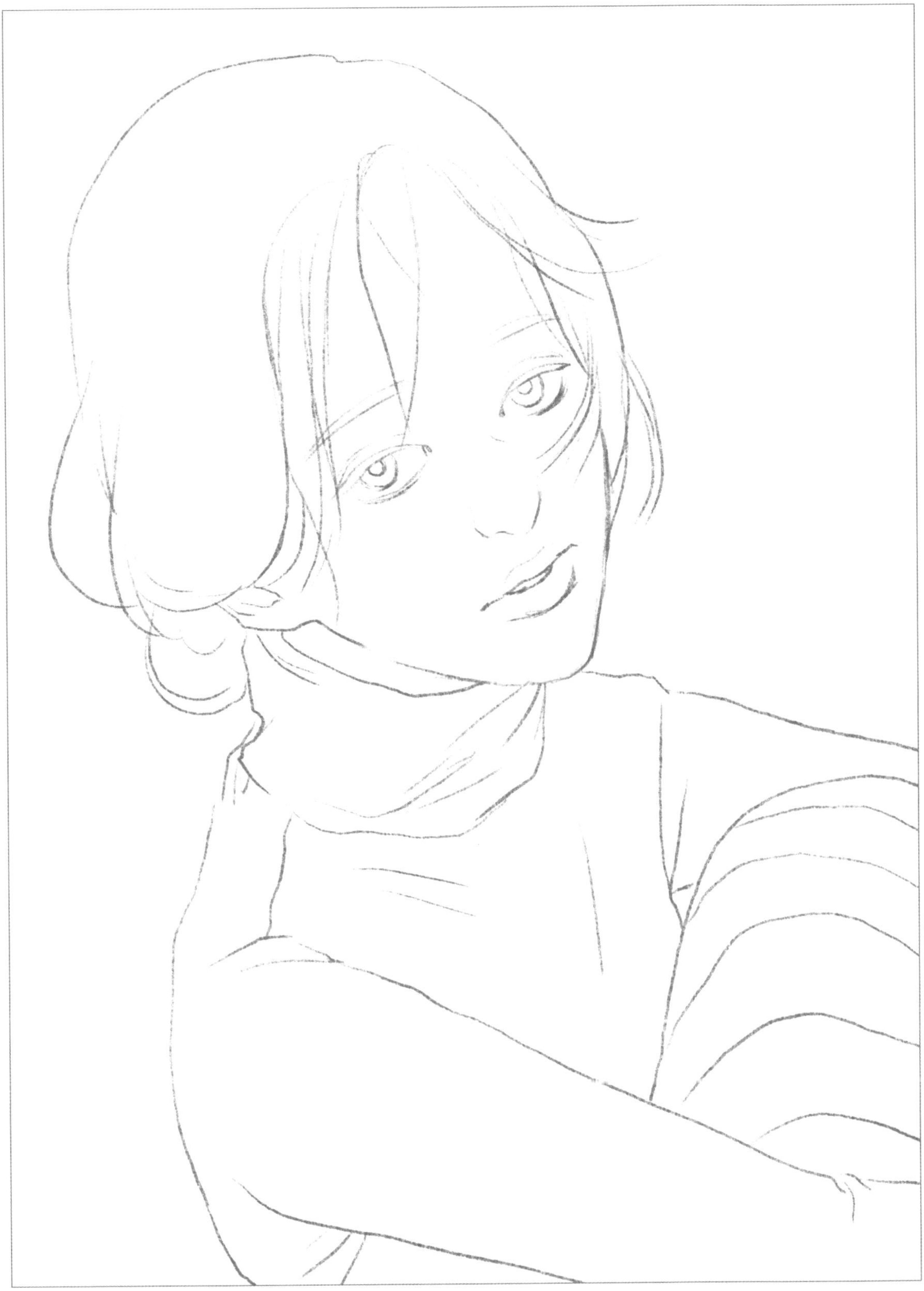

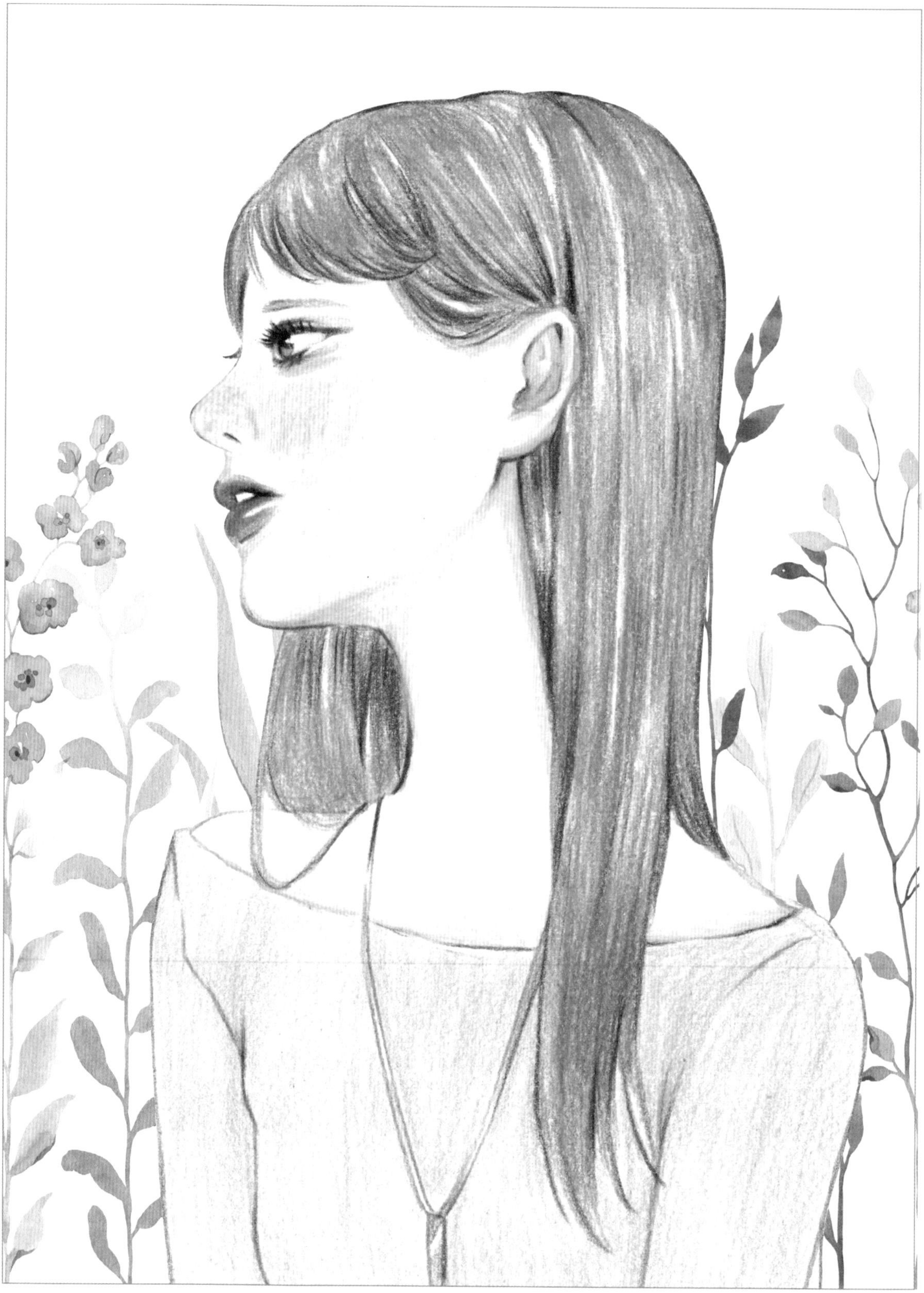

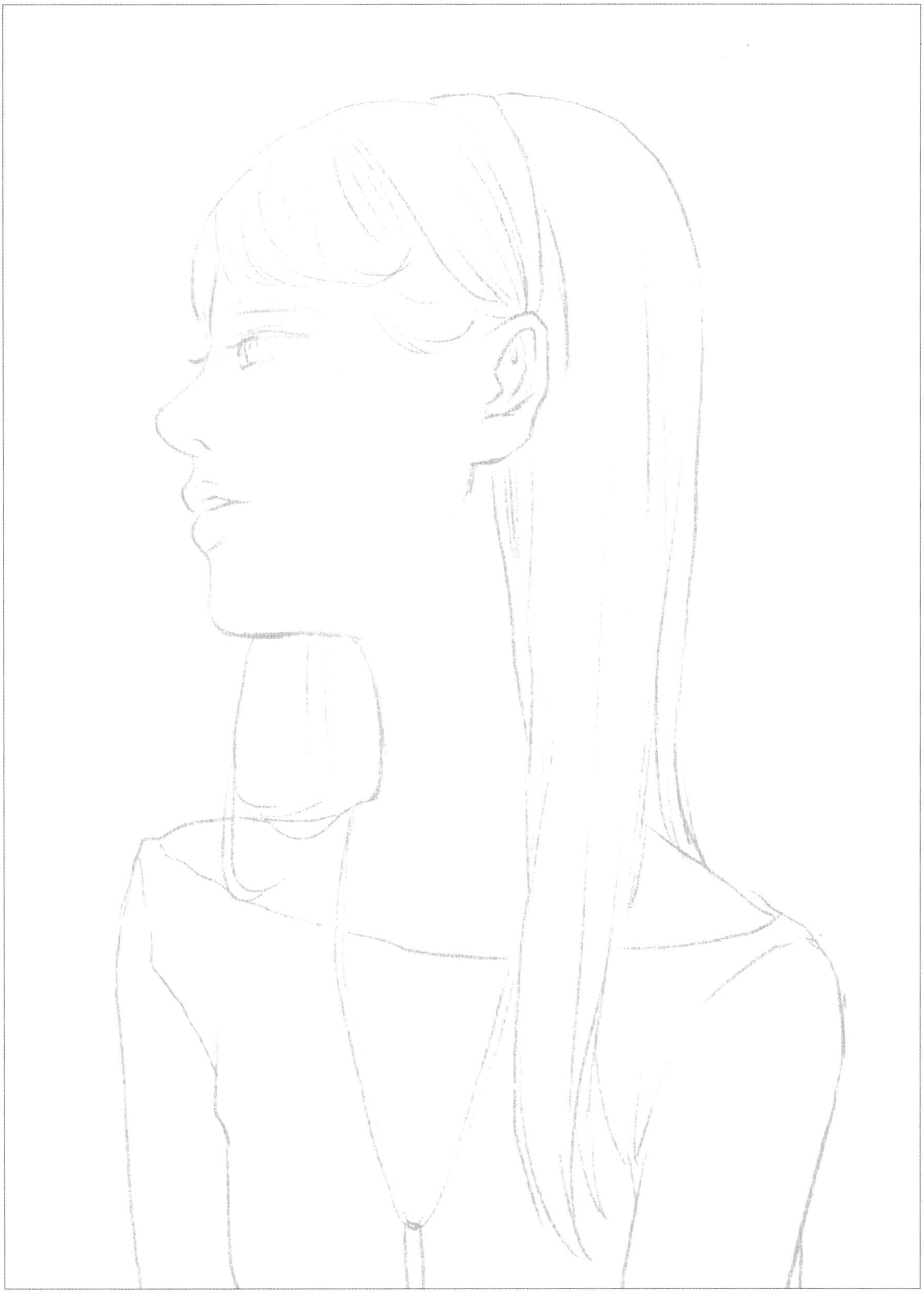

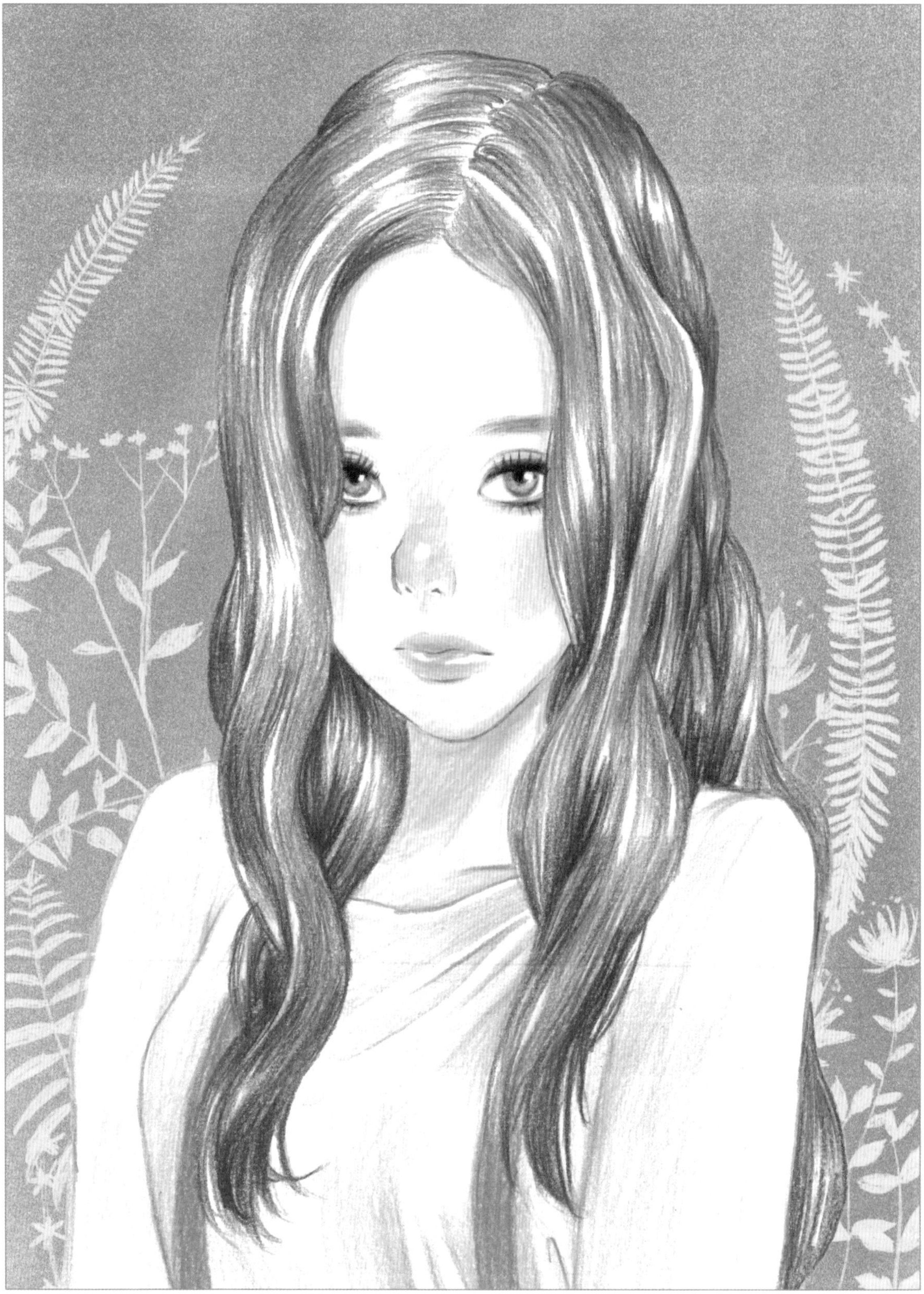

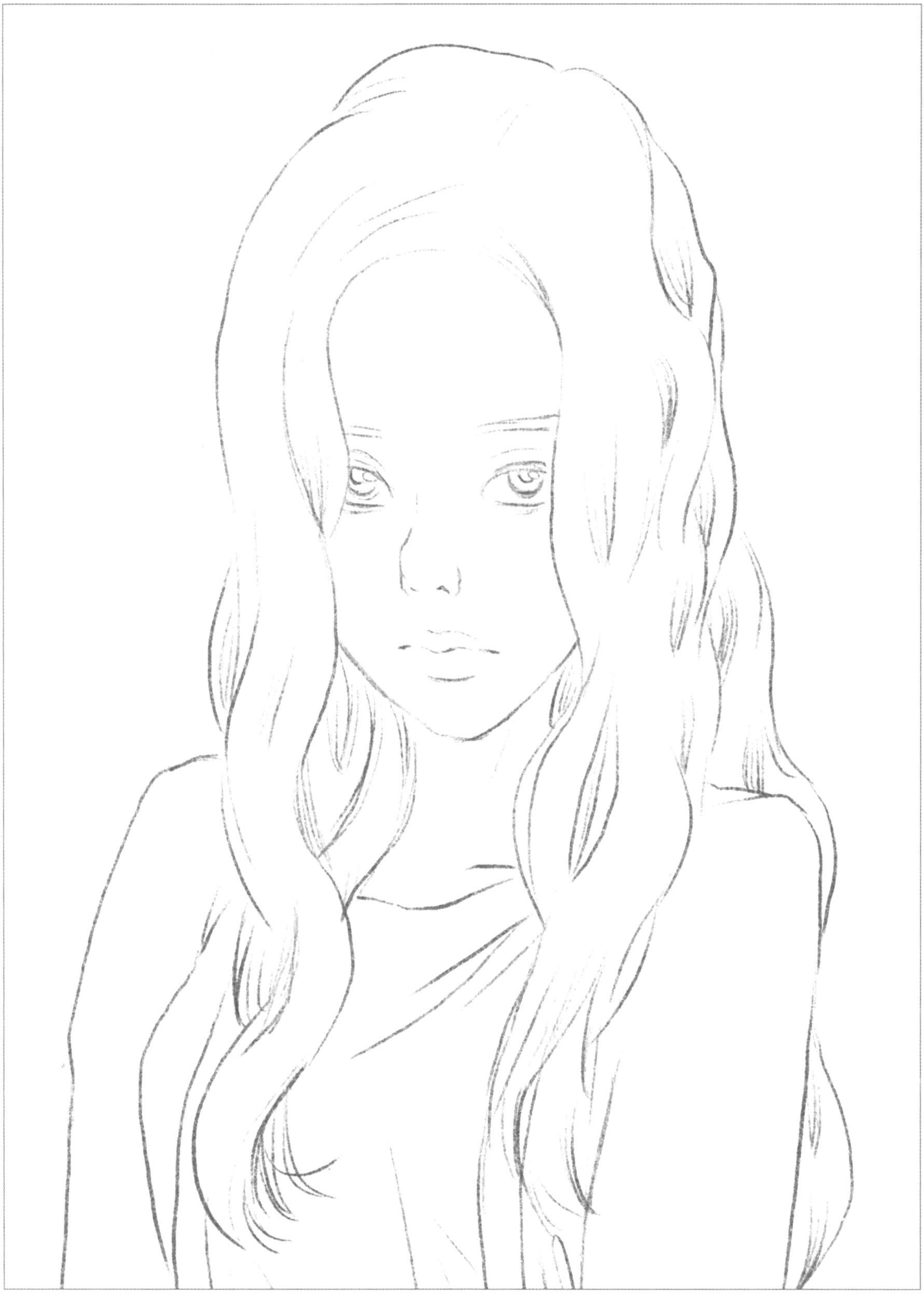

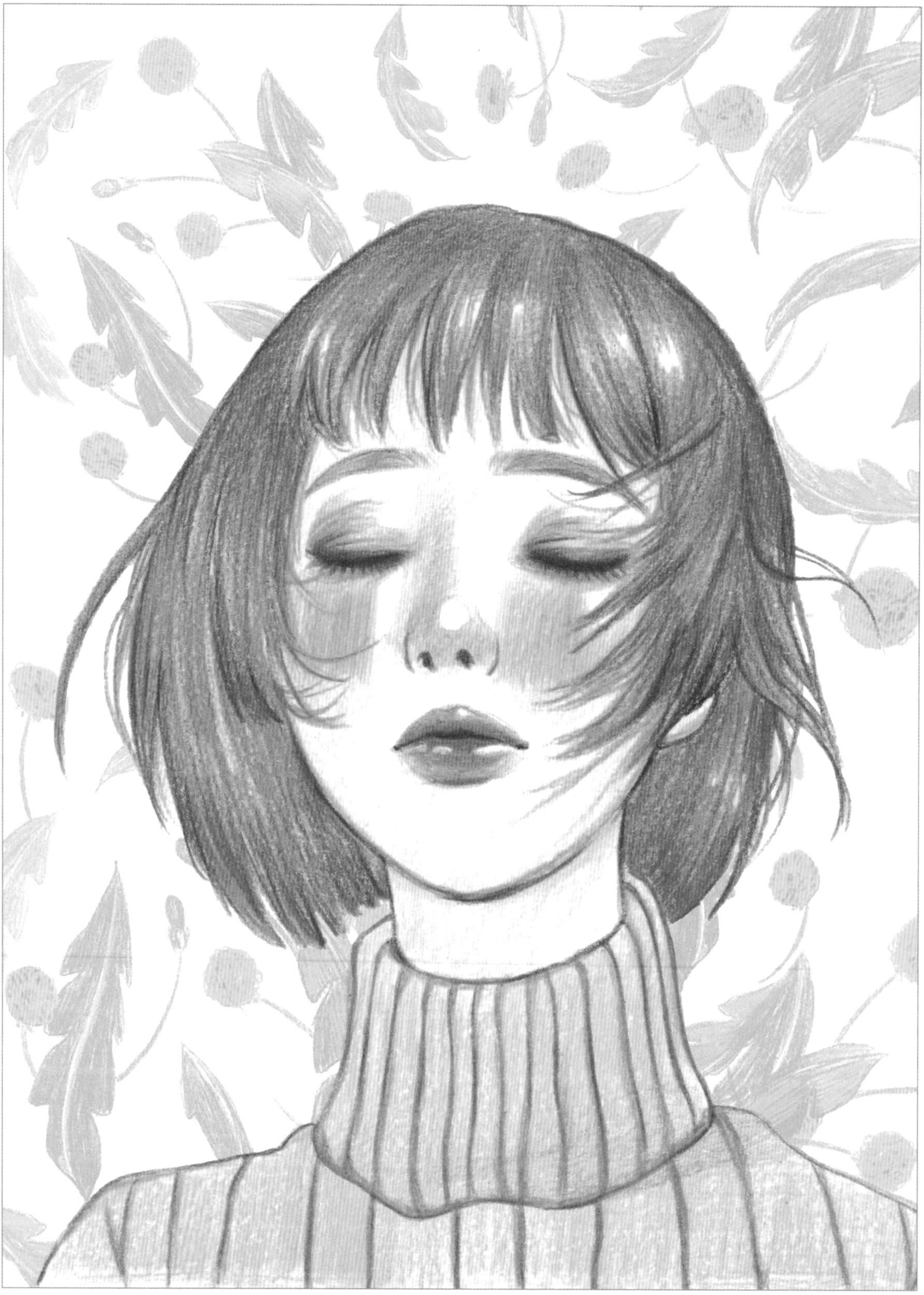

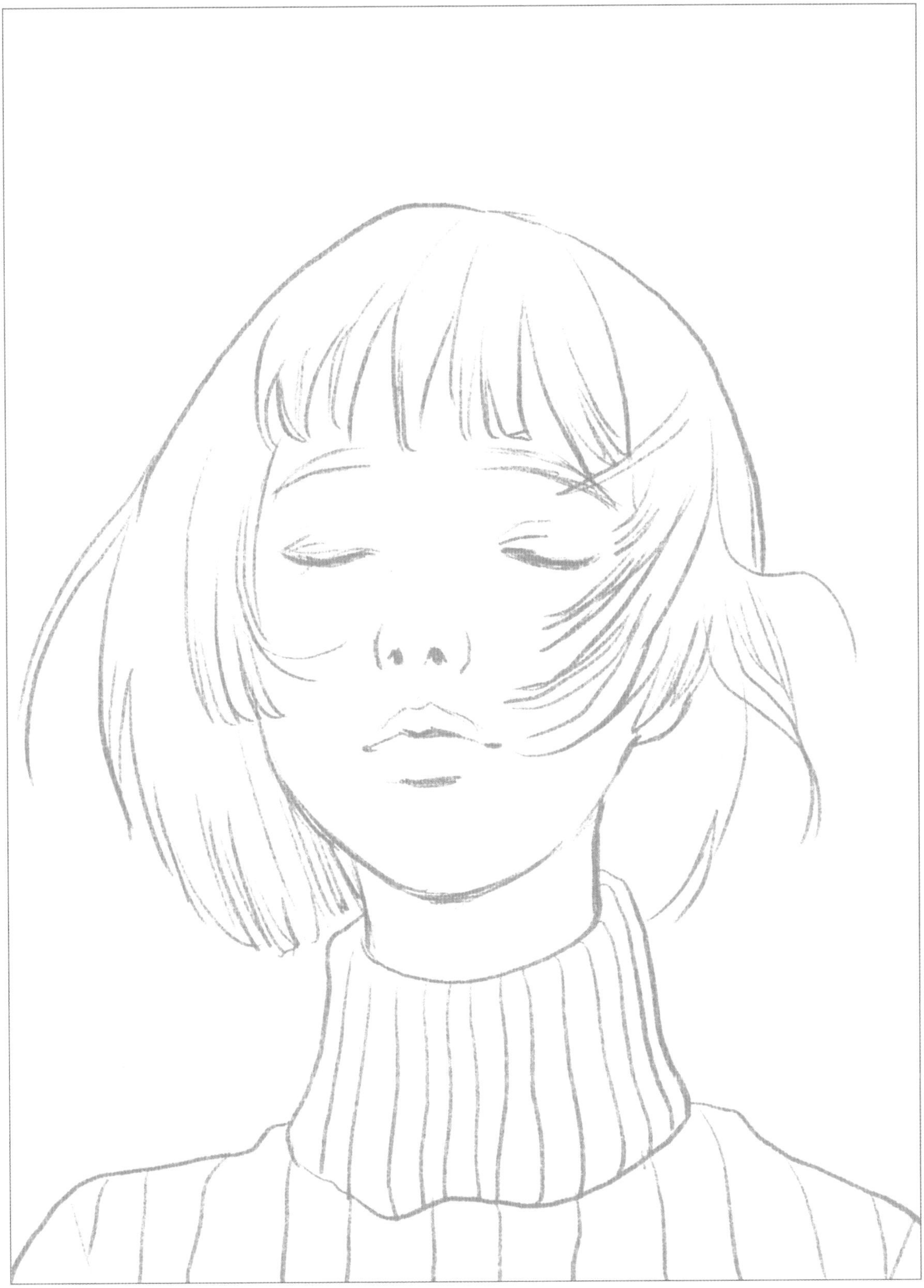

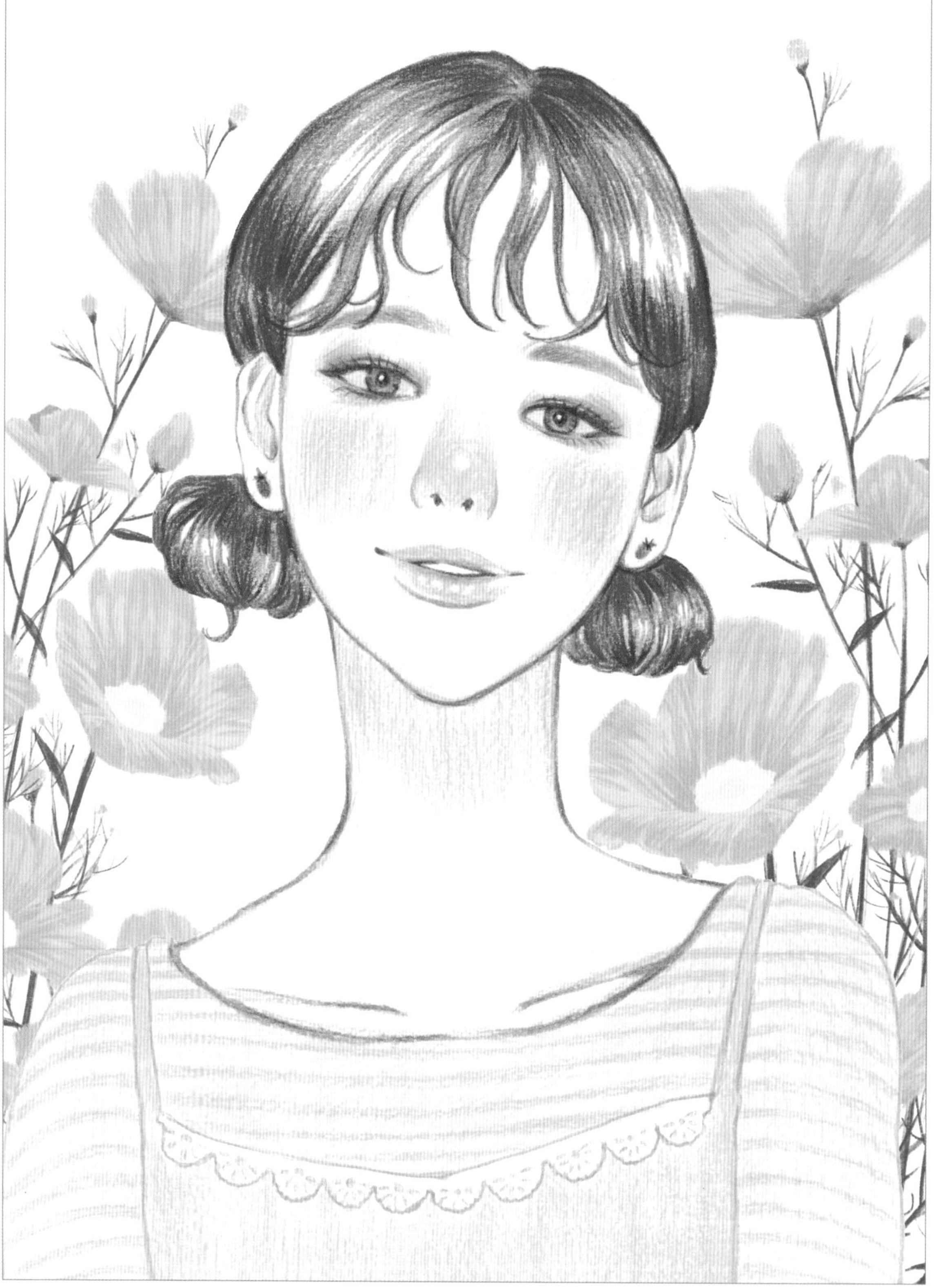

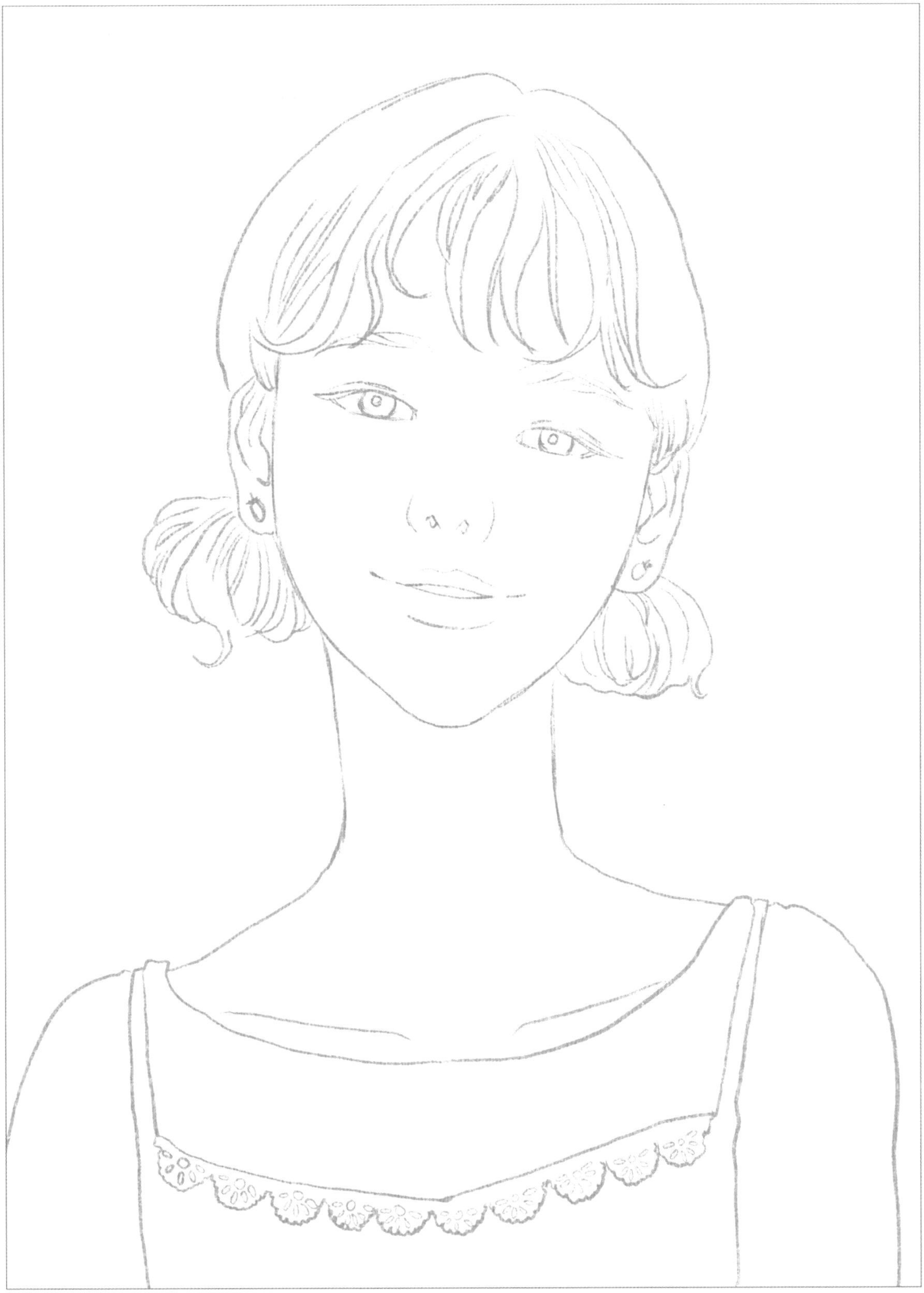

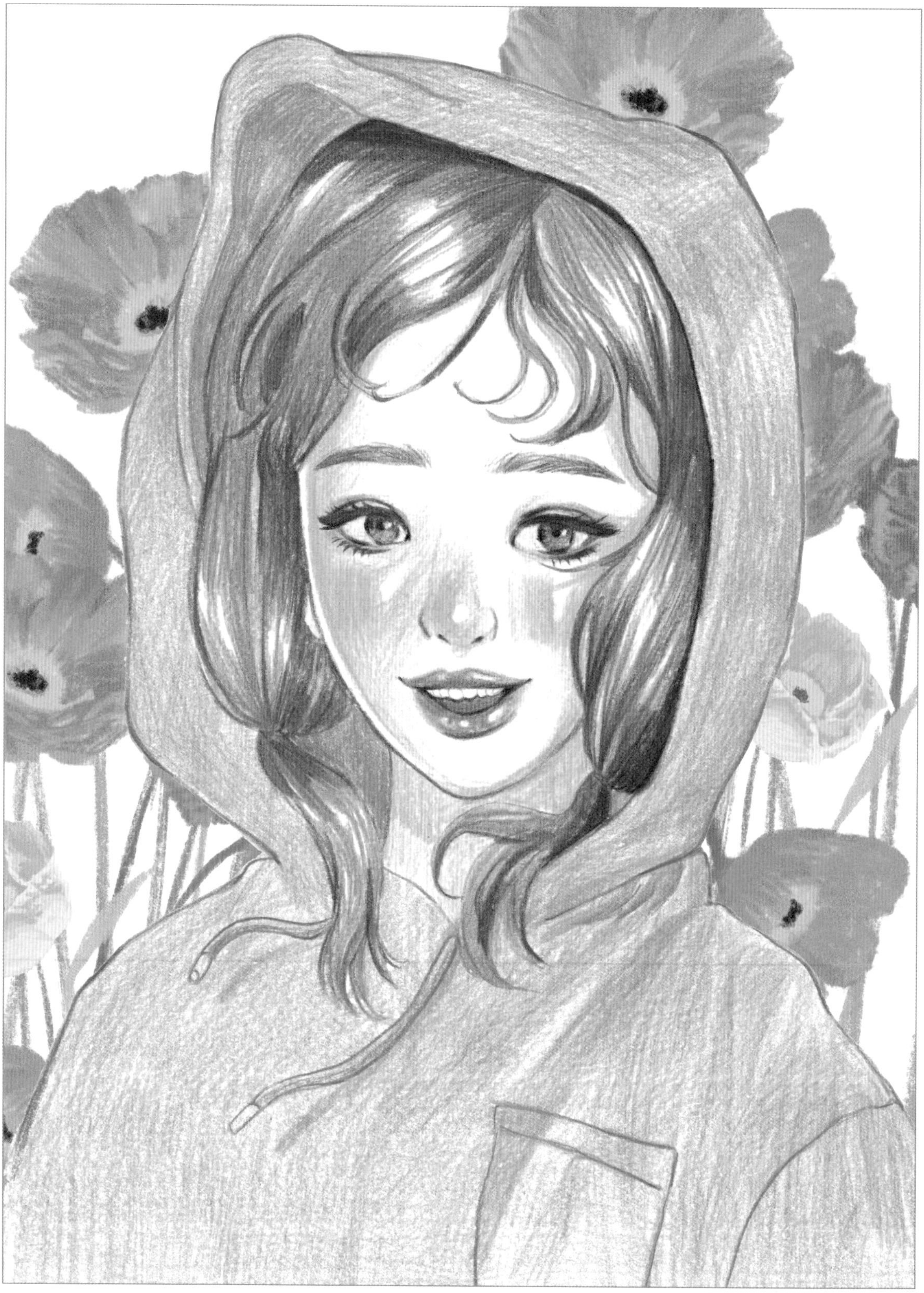

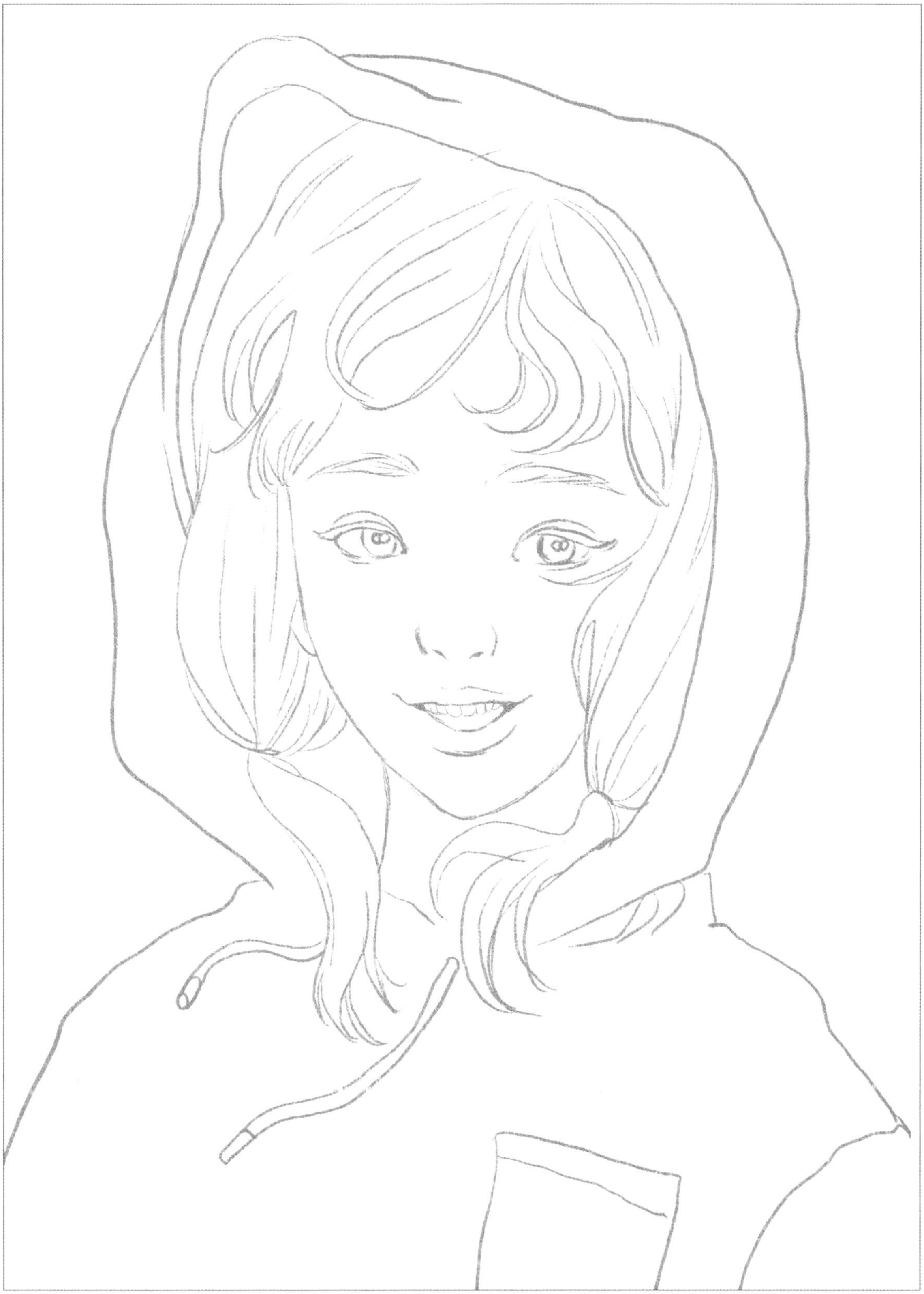

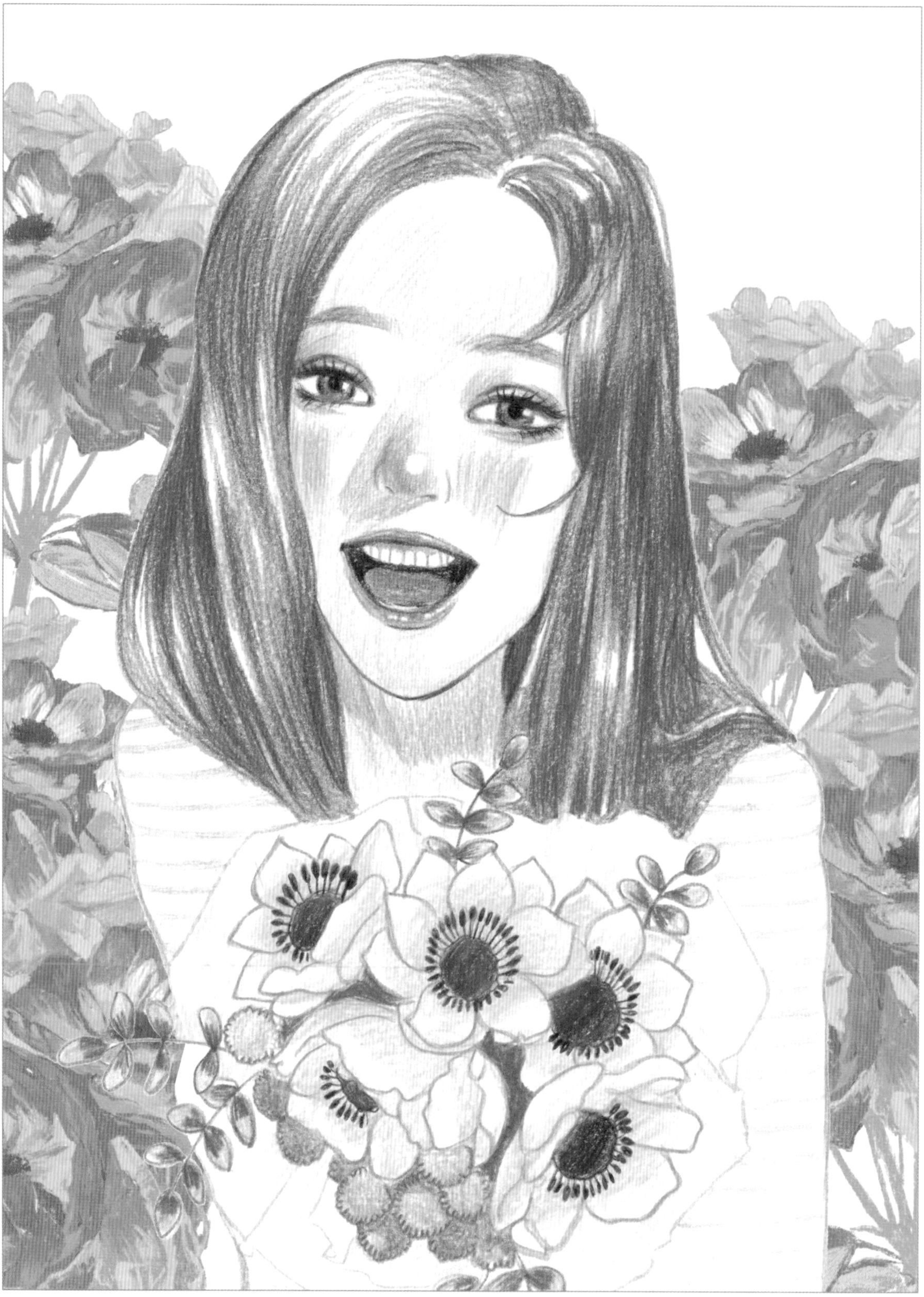

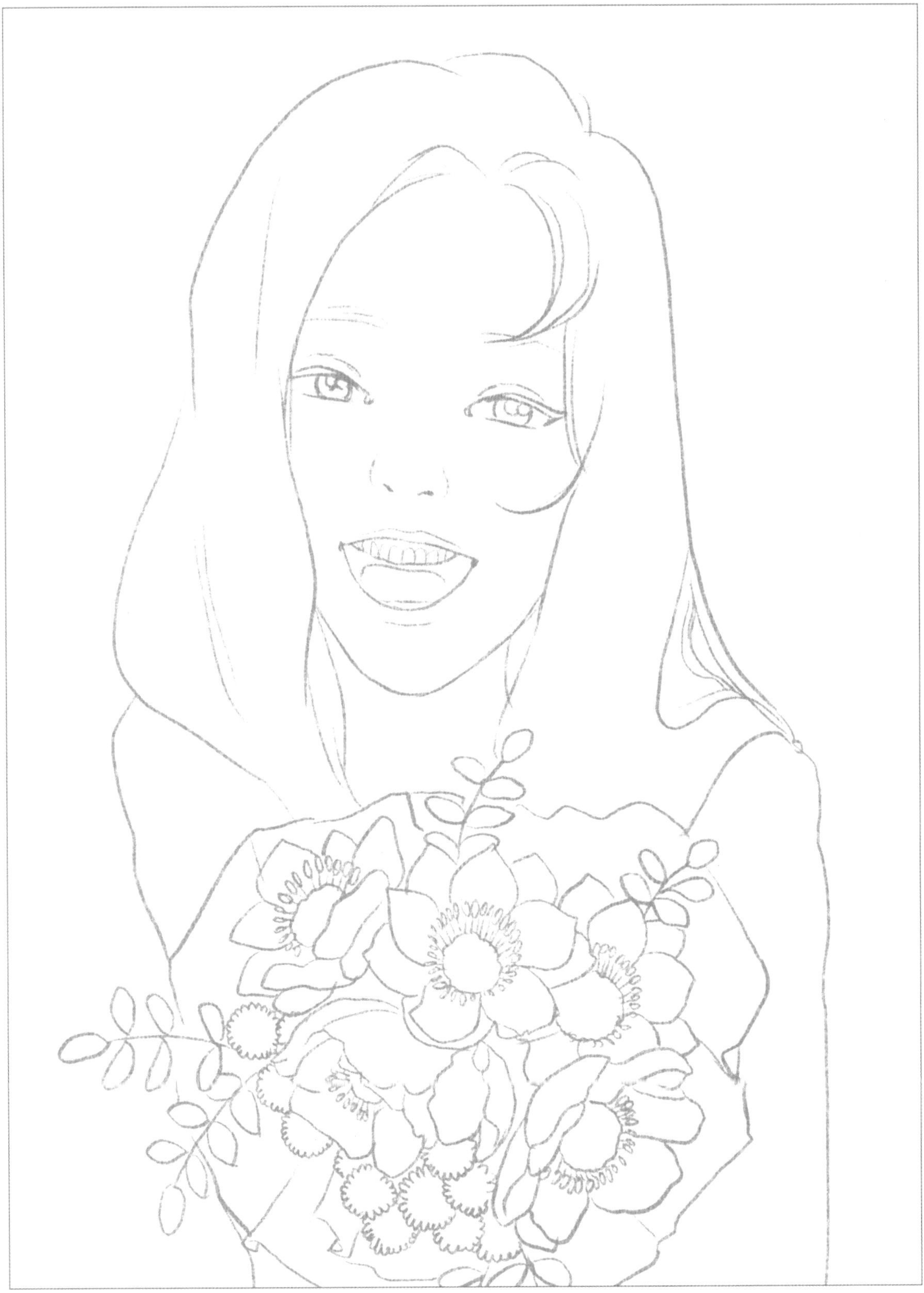

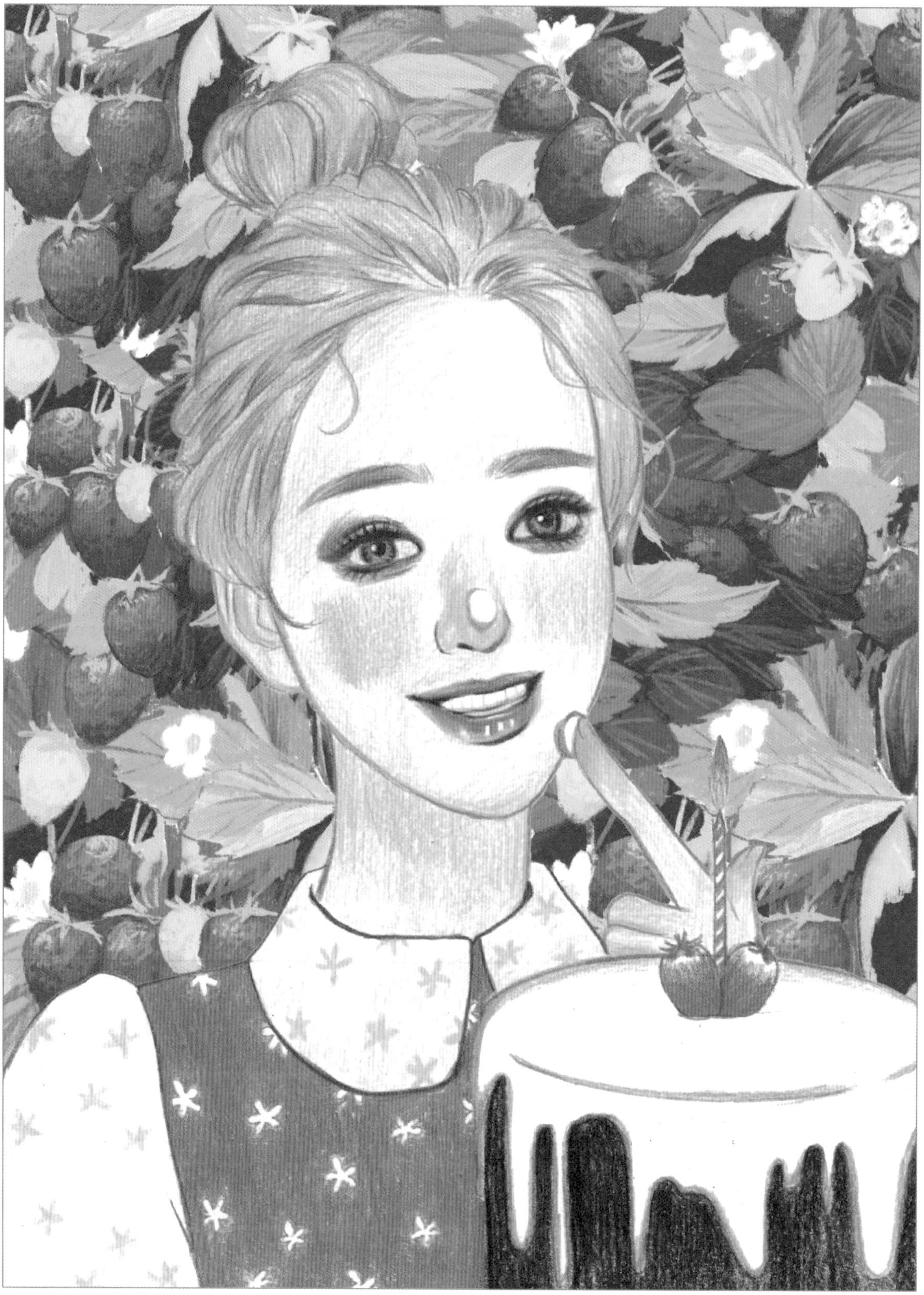

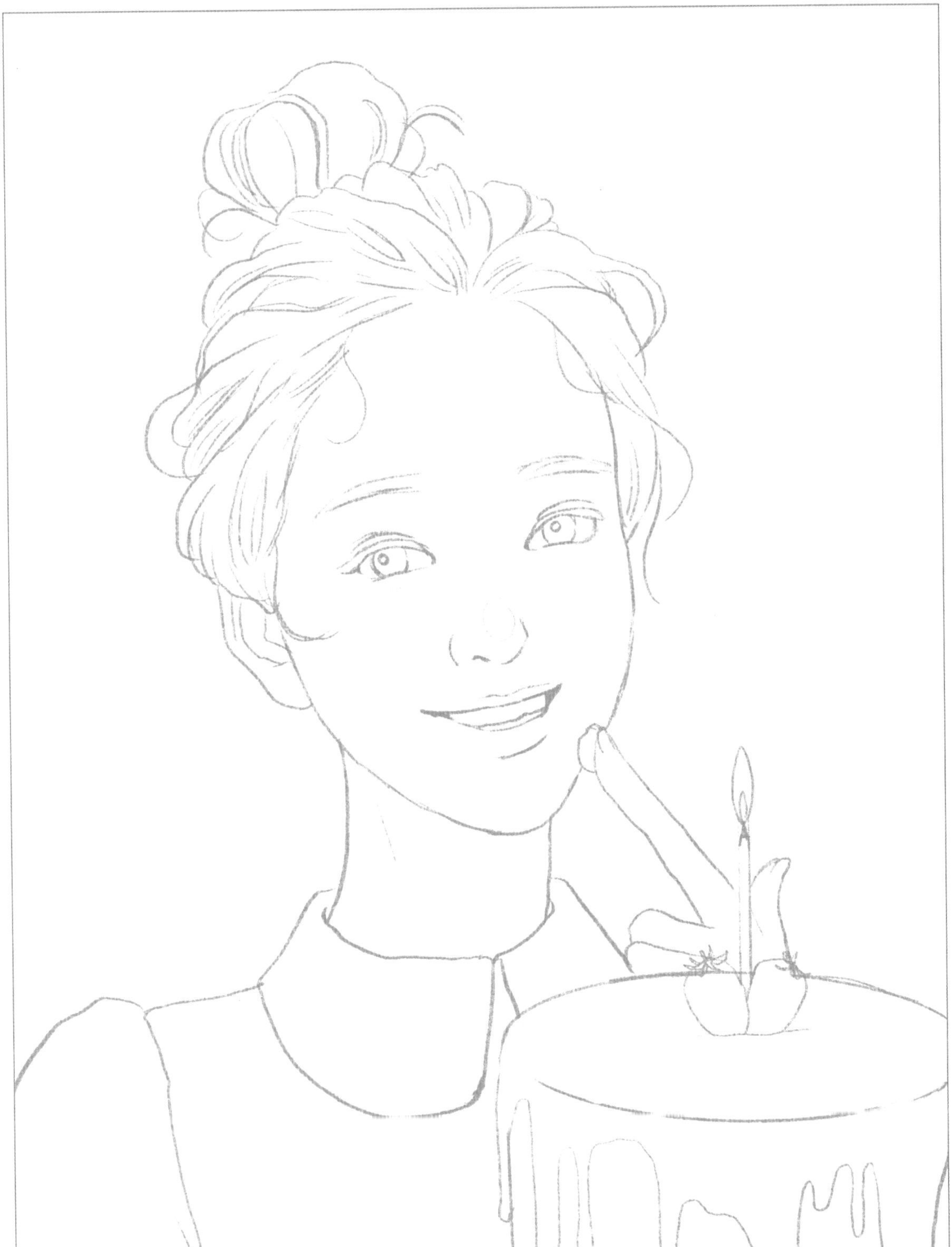

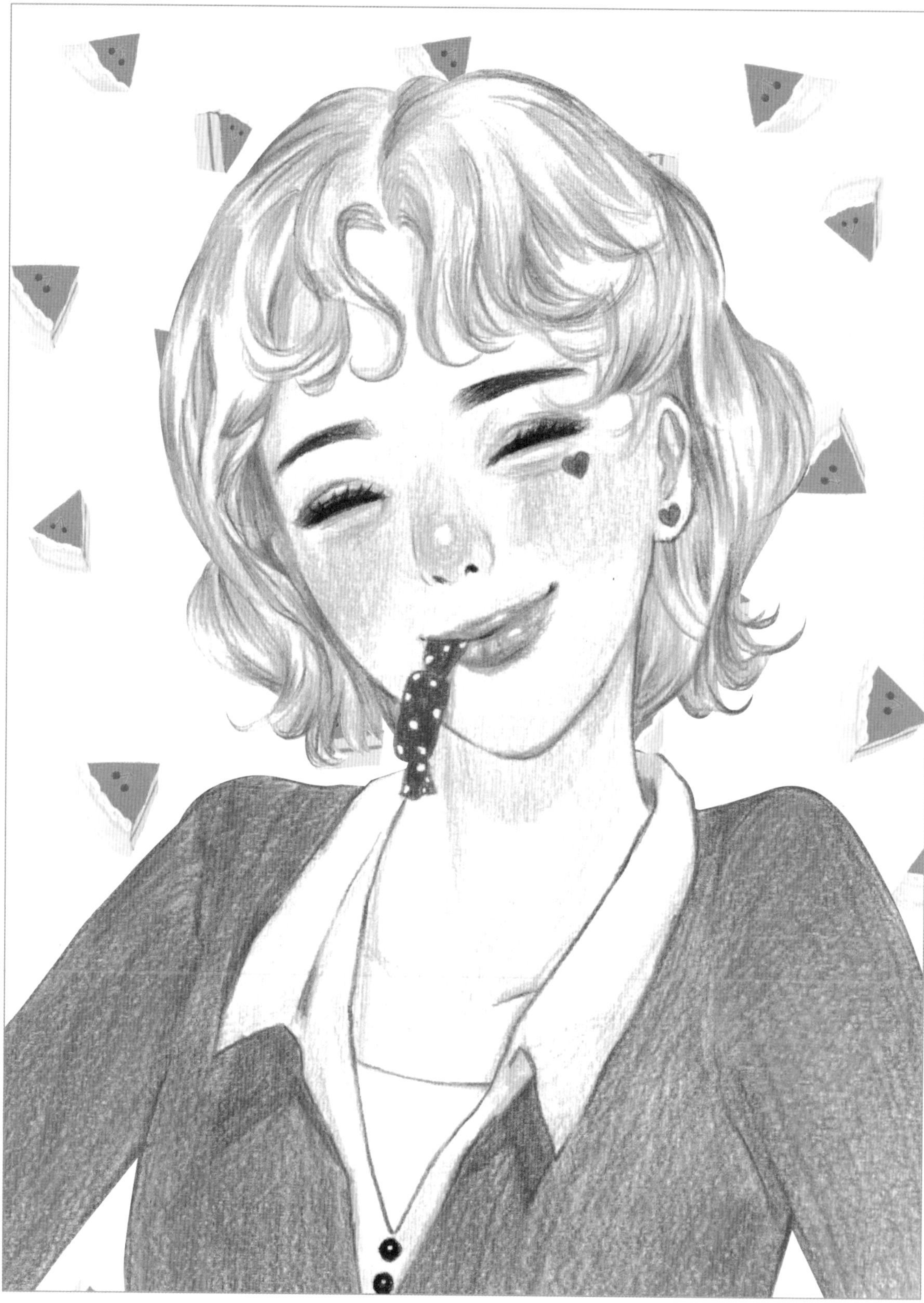

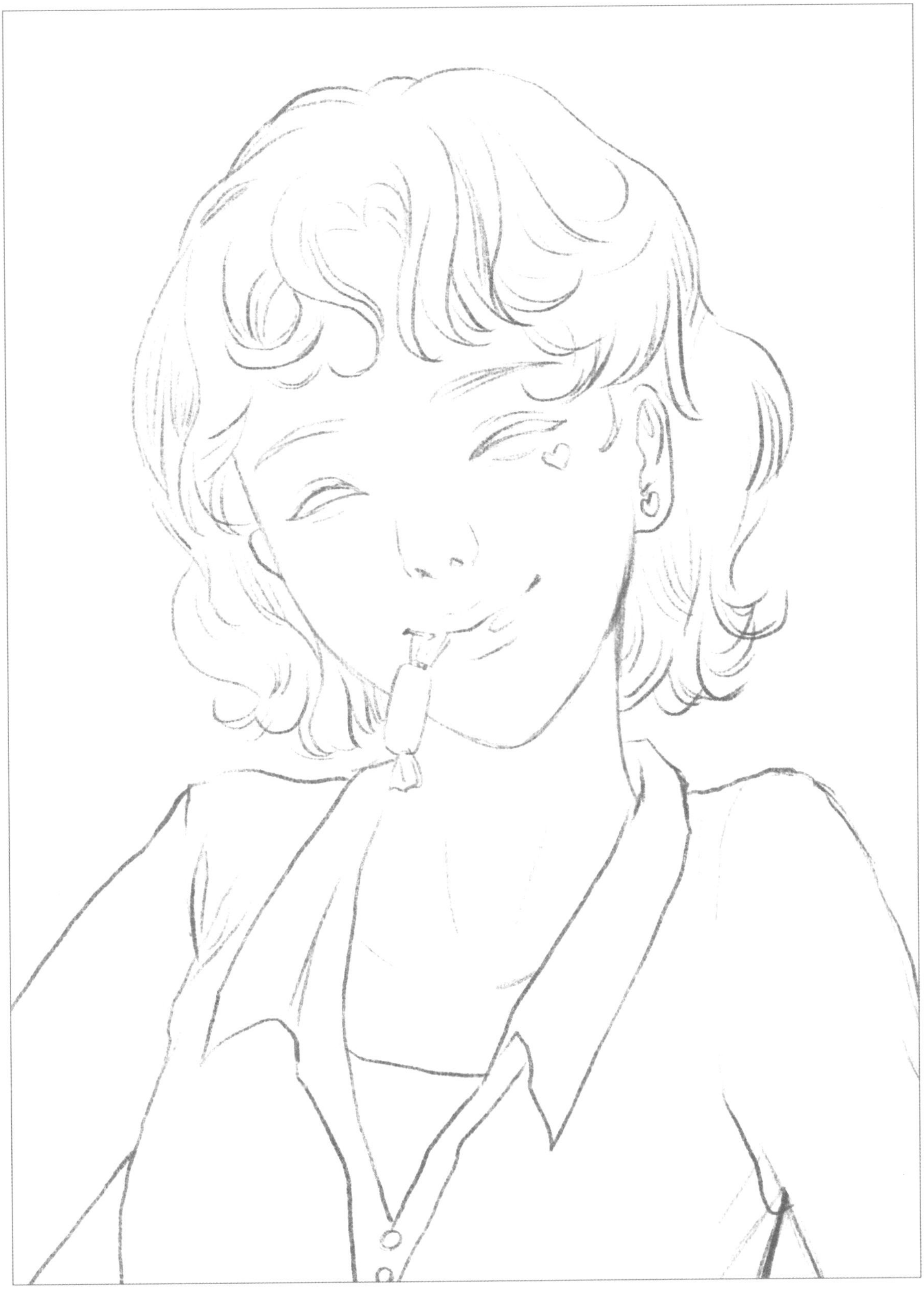

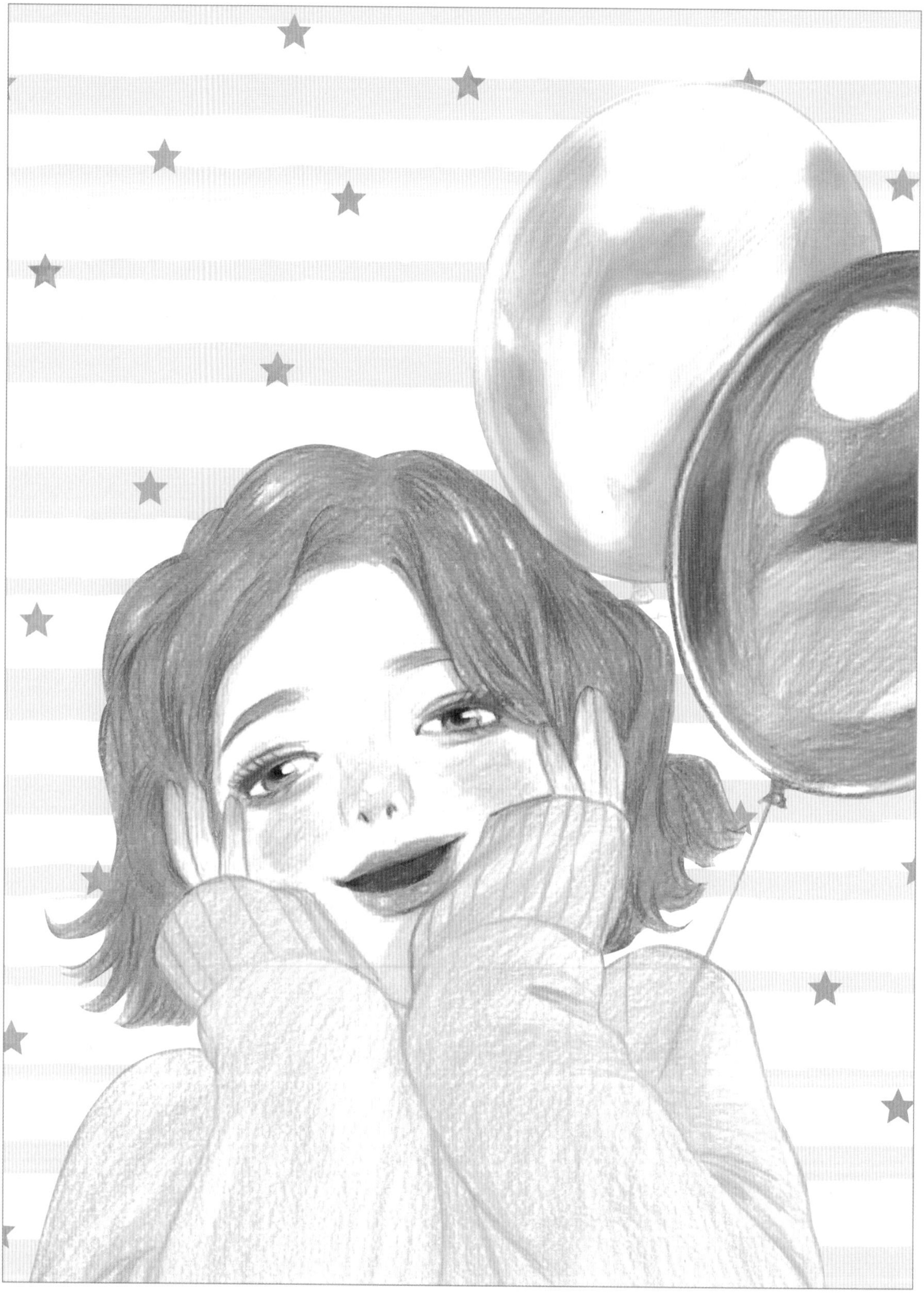

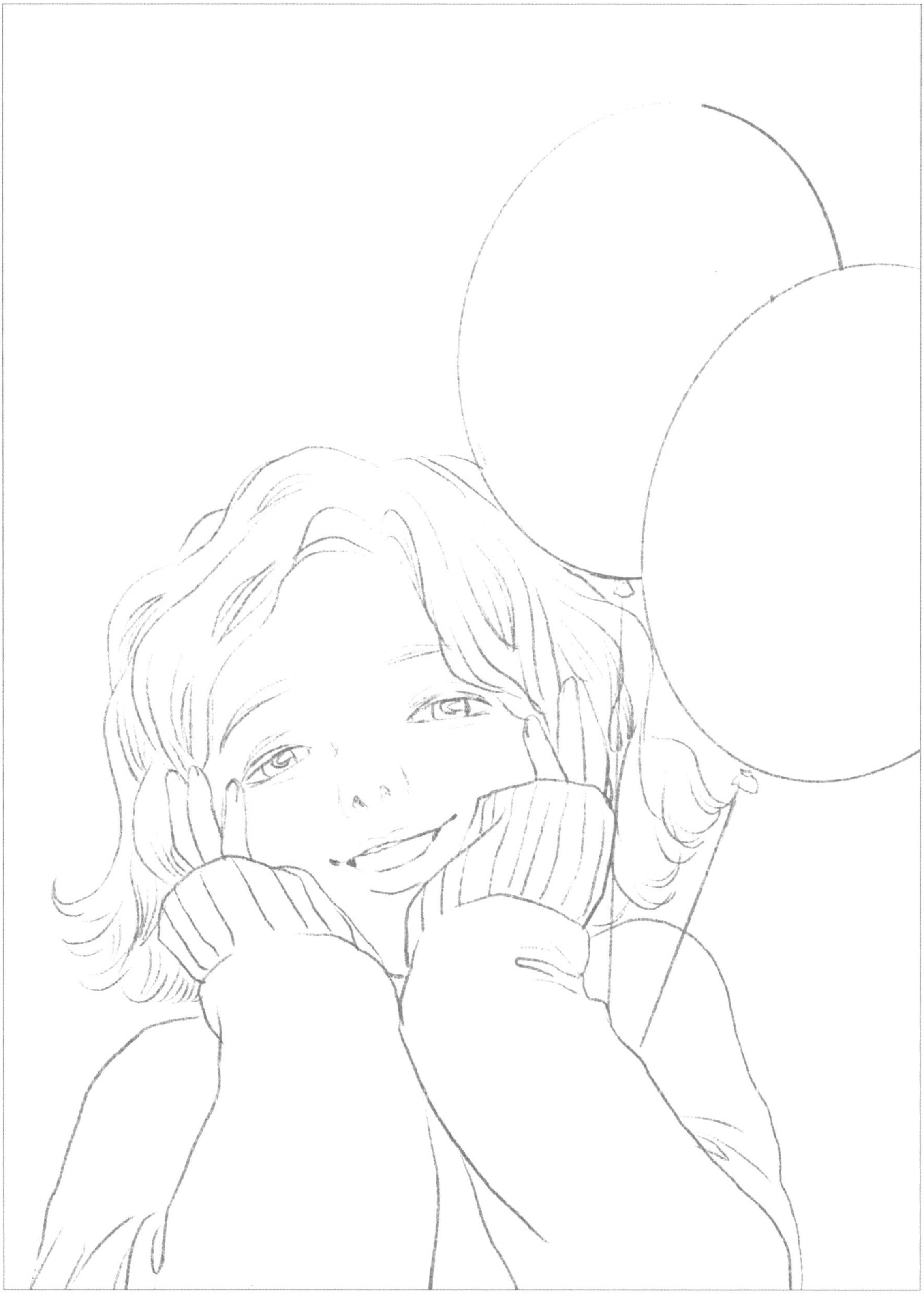

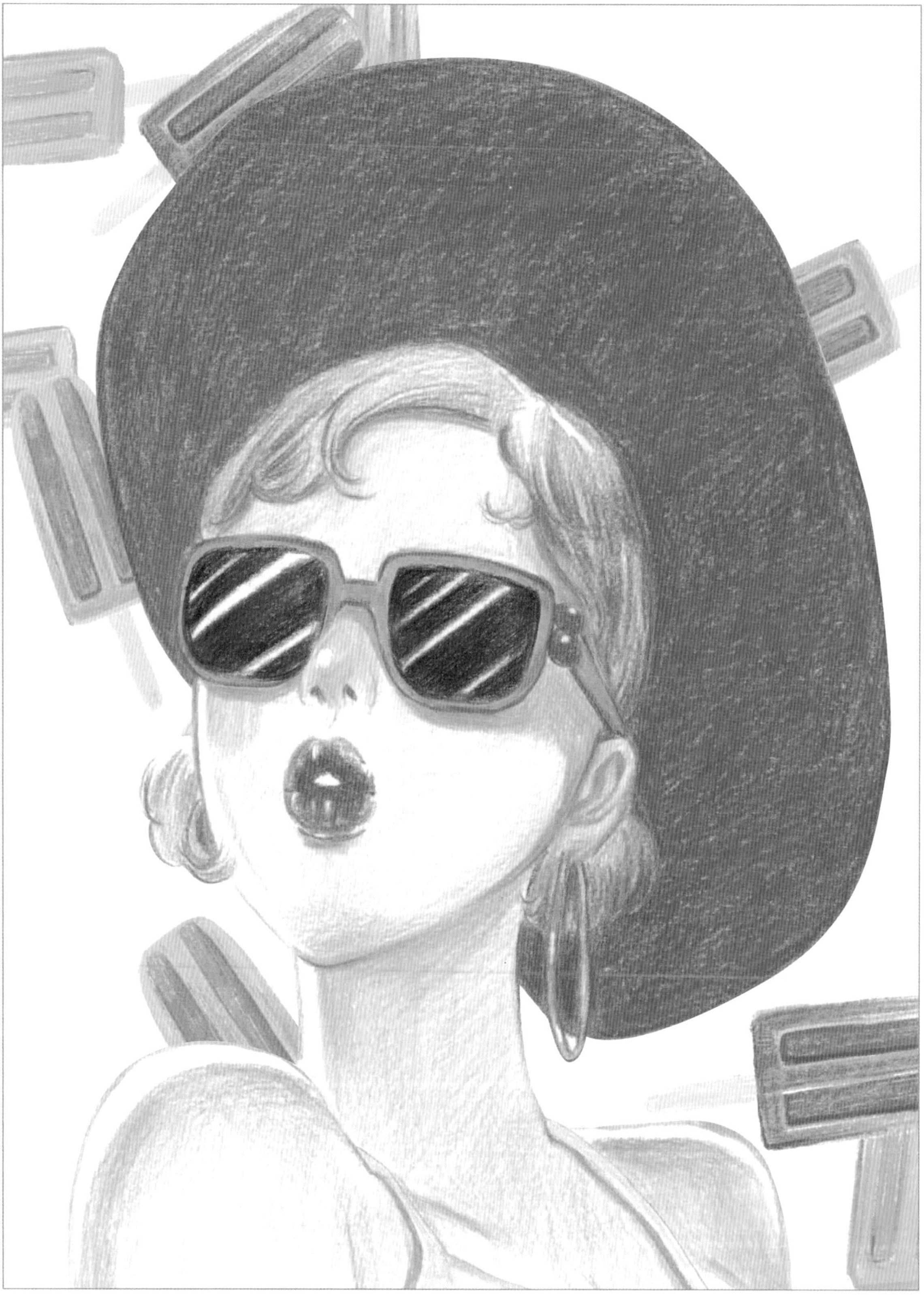

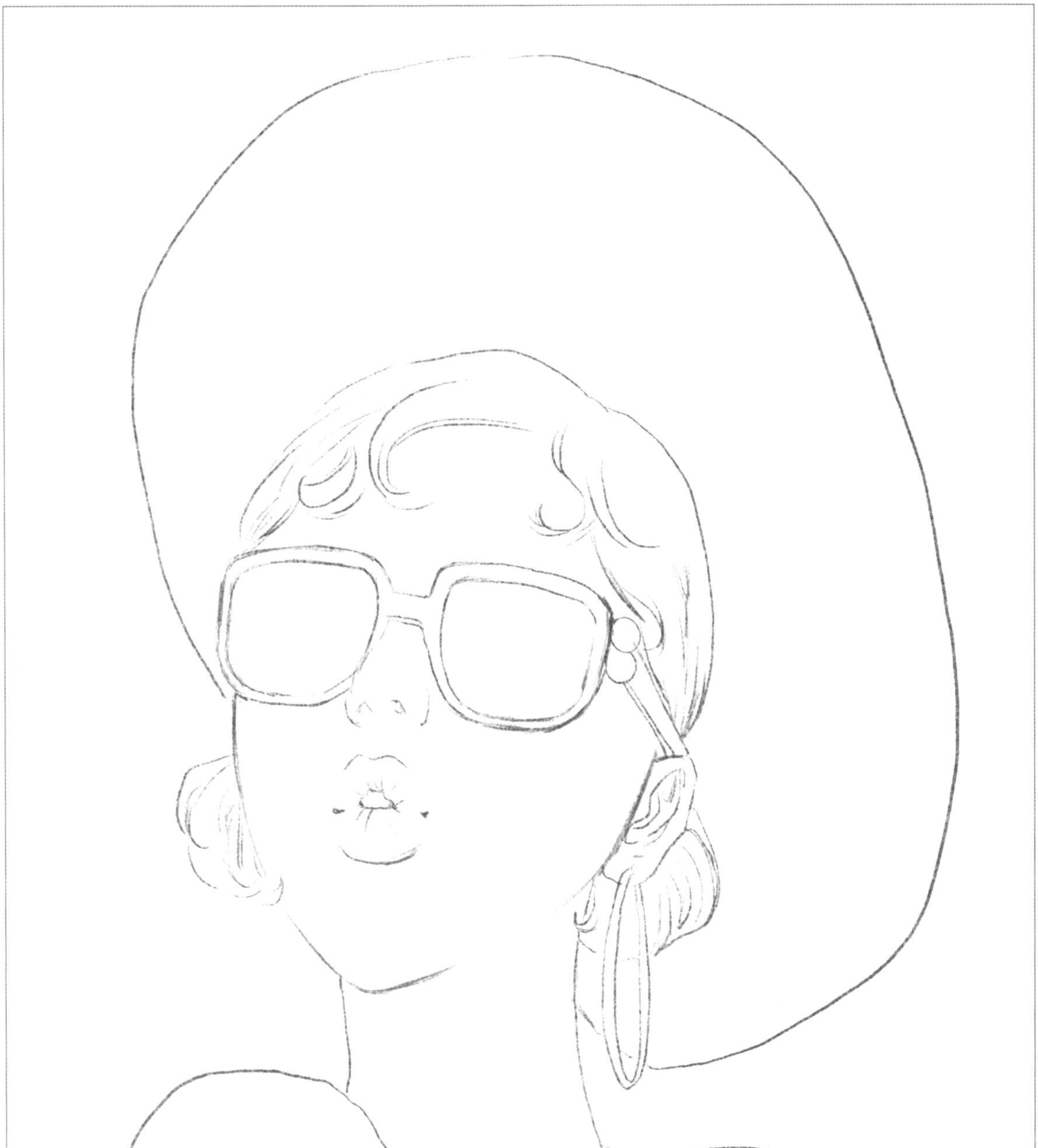